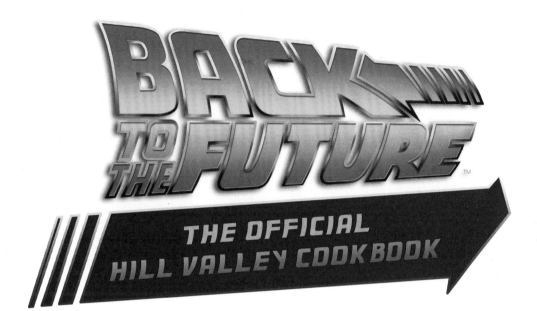

BACK TO THE FUTURE

THE OFFICIAL
HILL VALLEY COOKBOOK

BACK TO THE FUTURE™

THE OFFICIAL HILL VALLEY COOKBOOK

OVER **65** CLASSIC HILL VALLEY RECIPES
FROM THE PAST, PRESENT, AND FUTURE!

Written by Allison Robicelli
Recipes by Matt Robicelli

Photos by Ted Thomas

TITAN BOOKS

London

An Insight Editions book

CONTENTS

ALTERNATE 1985

1885

INTRODUCTION

The Back to the Future trilogy has just about everything you want in a movie series: excitement, adventure, laughter, romance, and . . . food: a surprising amount of delicious, hilarious ("Welcome Home, Uncle Joey!") food, as a matter of fact.

How many of us have wondered if the future might actually find us noshing on rehydrated pizzas? Who among us has watched George attempting to win over Lorraine, his *destiny*, in Lou's Cafe without craving a classic grilled burger and rich milkshake? Isn't "own a voice-activated fruit robot" on *everyone's* bucket list? And what, exactly, does Wake-Up Juice taste like?

With this cookbook, you can travel through the ages of Hill Valley in your own kitchen, tasting the culinary delights of the times. Just like Marty and Doc, this book's dishes go as far back as the rough and tumble year of 1885 and as far forward as "the distant future of 2015," with a zany mix of dishes, drinks, and desserts from each of the core time periods.

Just like Marty and Doc, we begin our journey in the year 1985: a hectic, on-the-go age when people believed toaster pastries were a nutritious—and convenient—breakfast. We then explore the culinary experiments of the 1950s: comforting casseroles, soda fountain sips, and, of course, tasty and convenient TV dinners. While the real 2015 wasn't *quite* as the sequel predicted, that doesn't mean you can't cook up some retro-futuristic fun with a bevy of treats inspired by the unique vision we see in these timeless films. Then things get weird as we head to a terrifying alternate 1985 controlled by corrupt "businessman" Biff Tannen, where we'll be spending our time at the Pleasure Paradise Casino & Hotel buffet. Finally, we end our journey with grub inspired by the meals of the settlers of the Old West, just like Seamus and Maggie McFly.

We, the people of the future, may not have hoverboards, self-lacing sneakers, or dehydrated pizzas . . . yet, but we may just have the closest thing: this one-of-a-kind cookbook.

TIME-HONORED TOOLS, TECHNIQUES, AND TREATS

The world of cooking is as vast as the wide open spaces of the California frontier, but to get you started, here is a quick rundown of some of the tools, techniques, and treats (ingredients) you will need for the recipes in this book.

TOOLS

BAKING SHEET

Baking sheets, also known as sheet pans, are not the same thing as cookie sheets. Cookie sheets are rather flimsy on the bottom, which is fine for baking biscuits, scones, and (of course) cookies, but not much else. Baking sheets are heavier and sturdier. They're 18 inches wide and 13 inches long, with a high metal rim.

BISCUIT CUTTER

A good biscuit cutter must be sharp on one side to slice cleanly through dough without crimping edges, resulting in biscuits that are tall, light, and flaky. If you don't have a cutter, use a glass that has thin sides, like a wineglass. Avoid anything with a thick rim, like mugs or pint glasses, which will smush the edges and give you flatter, denser biscuits.

CASSEROLE DISH

Casserole dishes come in many different sizes, which can be confusing. The casseroles in this book work in a 9-by-13-inch baking dish or a 2-quart casserole dish. If your baking or casserole dishes are a bit larger or smaller than the one called for, the recipes will still work. Just make sure to keep a close watch while the food is in the oven as the differently sized vessel may alter the cooking time.

CAST IRON SKILLET

A cast iron skillet ain't just for cowboys—in fact, it's one of the best all-purpose tools you can have in your kitchen. Cast iron gets hot and *stays* hot, and the more you cook with it, the more nonstick it becomes. It can be used on the stovetop as a skillet or in the oven as a baking dish, and sometimes it acts as both in the same meal. Never, *ever* put your cast iron skillet in the dishwasher; scrub it out with soapy water and a dishcloth or brush, then dry thoroughly on the stovetop to make sure any excess water evaporates. Rub it gently with a paper towel and a quarter teaspoon of oil.

DEEP-FRY THERMOMETER

This tool is absolutely essential if you're deep-frying, since you'll need to raise and reduce your heat throughout the cooking process to keep the oil between 350° and 375°F. If the thermometer reads too high, your food will burn; if too low, your food will be greasy. Select a thermometer that's easy to read and that clips to the side of the pot without resting on the bottom.

DUTCH OVEN

Back in 1885, most frontier citizens cooked in Dutch ovens made by local blacksmiths (such as Dr. Emmett Brown). Here in the 21st century, we *still* cook in Dutch ovens, as did many moms in 1985 and many more grandmas in 1955. The reason this pot is so timeless is that there's almost nothing you can't cook with it. Use it for soups and stews, long-simmering sauces, deep-frying, roasting, or braising. It worked for the simpler meals in the McFly farm kitchen, and it'll work for the more elaborate ones in yours.

MASON JARS

Mason jars range in size from 4 ounces, which hold half a cup to gallon-size that can hold a whole lotta jelly. If you're making Maggie McFly's Cider Jelly (page 111), use whatever size jars you like—perhaps you want to gift some to your neighbors, or maybe you'd rather save it all for yourself. Whatever the case, remember that if you're intending to store your jelly for the long term, visit the website of your jars' manufacturer for detailed directions on hot water canning.

PIPING BAGS AND TIPS

If you want to make a parole cake for Uncle Joey that looks as "good" as the one in the movie, you'll definitely need some small piping bags, which usually come in a set with decorating tips. You can buy these in most supermarket baking aisles.

STAND MIXER

In Marty's 2015, it seemed like every kitchen had a food rehydrator; in the real 2015, many kitchens boasted a stand mixer. With a motor much more powerful than that of a handheld mixer, stand mixers allow home cooks to quickly whip up thick batters, knead sturdy doughs, and prepare in minutes the sorts of dishes it took Maggie McFly hours to create.

TECHNIQUES

BROWN

When cooking meat, the first step is almost always to brown it. This is when meat develops much of its flavor. Brown your meat in a hot pan (preferably cast iron) with enough oil to slick the bottom. For non-ground meat, once you put it in the pan, *do not touch it* for four to five minutes, because moving the meat around will prevent it from getting a good sear. When it's time to flip the meat, if it's sticking to the pan, leave it for another minute or two—it will release on its own once it is brown enough. As for the color, it should be a beautiful deep amber brown.

CUT BUTTER

This technique is essential for making flaky biscuits and pie dough, and the most important rule to remember is that the butter must *always* be cold. First, *cut* the amount of butter that's called for in the recipe into small pieces about the size of a chickpea, then toss them in the dry ingredients (like flour) and smash with the back of a fork to *cut* them into even smaller pieces. If the butter starts to soften, pop the bowl in the freezer for 5 minutes to firm it up again.

DEEP-FRY

You don't need a special appliance to deep-fry, as long as you have a Dutch oven, a deep-fry thermometer, and cooking oil. Never deep-fry in olive oil; use canola or vegetable oil, which have a high smoke point and won't impart any off-tasting flavors to your food.

FLOAT

This is bartender-speak for pouring different liquors into a glass in such a way that they float on top of one another in separate layers. To do this, each liquor is slowly poured over the back of a spoon, so it flows into the glass gently. It can take a while to master this technique, so don't worry if you don't get it quite right on the first shot.

SHRED

There are many ways to shred a variety of foods. You can use a food processor with its included shredding/grating attachment, which works well for firm vegetables like carrots. You can use a handheld cheese grater, which is good for, well, cheese. If shredding cooked meat, like chicken or pulled pork, use your hands, two forks, or a stand mixer on low speed. And for more delicate foods, like cabbage, the best way to shred is by cutting thin strips with a very sharp knife.

TWIST

A twist is a small piece of citrus peel without the bitter white pith. You can easily make one with a vegetable peeler, then cut your citrus peel into thin pieces using a sharp knife.

TREATS (INGREDIENTS)

EDIBLE GOLD LEAF

Yes, edible gold leaf is *actually* gold, and, yes, it is 100 percent edible! Gold leaf is flavorless, so it's not used for taste but rather for presentation. Lining your martini glass with it for a Number One Citizen cocktail (page 93) won't make it more delicious, but it will make you feel like a high roller at the Pleasure Paradise Casino.

GOCHUJANG

This Korean condiment is a fermented chile paste that is simultaneously sweet, savory, and spicy. It's got a fiery umami taste that's as explosive as plutonium, and once you try it, you'll want to find ways to sneak it into everything.

MALT POWDER

Every soda fountain has a can of dry malted milk behind the counter, and for good reason. This flavor enhancer is a mixture of milk and barley malt extract, which is then dehydrated and ground into powder. It was originally created to be mixed with water to make malted milk, but its purpose changed when someone discovered it's even better when stirred into milkshakes.

MASCARPONE

Mascarpone is absolutely essential in tiramisu, and can easily be found in your supermarket's fine cheese section. This Italian cream cheese has twice as much butterfat as American cream cheese, giving it the taste of fresh, sweet cream without a trace of tartness. It's a richer, more luscious cheese, which is everything you want in your tiramisu.

PIE CRUST

There are two different pie crusts called for in this book. Some recipes, like Quiche Lorraine (page 90), require a frozen pre-molded crust, which comes fully formed in a pie pan (you can also use your favorite pie crust recipe if you choose). Others, like the Exploding Candy Toaster Tarts (page 61), use refrigerated pie dough, which is pre-rolled but not pre-shaped, and comes in a package of two sheets.

PUFF PASTRY

If you took a microscope to puff pastry, you'd see that it is made up of *dozens* of ultra-thin layers of fat, water, and flour; when it bakes, the water evaporates into steam, causing the layers to "puff" up. There are two kinds you can find in the frozen section: all-butter puff pastry, and shortening puff pastry. If you have the option, always buy the all-butter version.

PIGNOLI

Pine nuts, also known as pignoli, are not actually nuts—they're seeds found inside pine cones! Compared with most nuts, they're a bit more expensive, but in Mr. Peabody's Pignoli Cookies (page 35), they're worth it.

SIMPLE SYRUP

Though simple syrup is available at the local liquor store, there's no reason not to make your own when it's literally just sugar and water. Pour an equal amount of each into a saucepan, bring it to a boil, stir until all the sugar is dissolved, and let cool completely.

SZECHUAN PEPPERCORNS

These peppercorns are very spicy, but in their own special, unique way. We usually associate spiciness with capsaicin, the fiery compound found in chile peppers. Szechuan peppercorns don't have any capsaicin, and they're not related to peppers or peppercorns. They're a seed husk that contains a molecule called hydroxy-alpha-sanshool. The name may not slip off the tongue, but you'll be set ablaze with a spicy heat that tingles until your lips go numb in a deliciously satisfying way. Trust us, it's not like anything else you have in your spice cabinet!

U-10 EXTRA COLOSSAL SHRIMP

If you've ever had shrimp cocktail at a fancy restaurant, chances are they were serving 21/25 Jumbo shrimp, which means there are 21 to 25 shrimp in a pound. For The World's Luckiest Shrimp Cocktail (page 89), you'll need U-10 Extra Colossal shrimp, which means there are fewer than 10 shrimp in a pound. Unfortunately, you won't find these massive shrimp in your supermarket's frozen-food section—you'll need to ask the fishmonger.

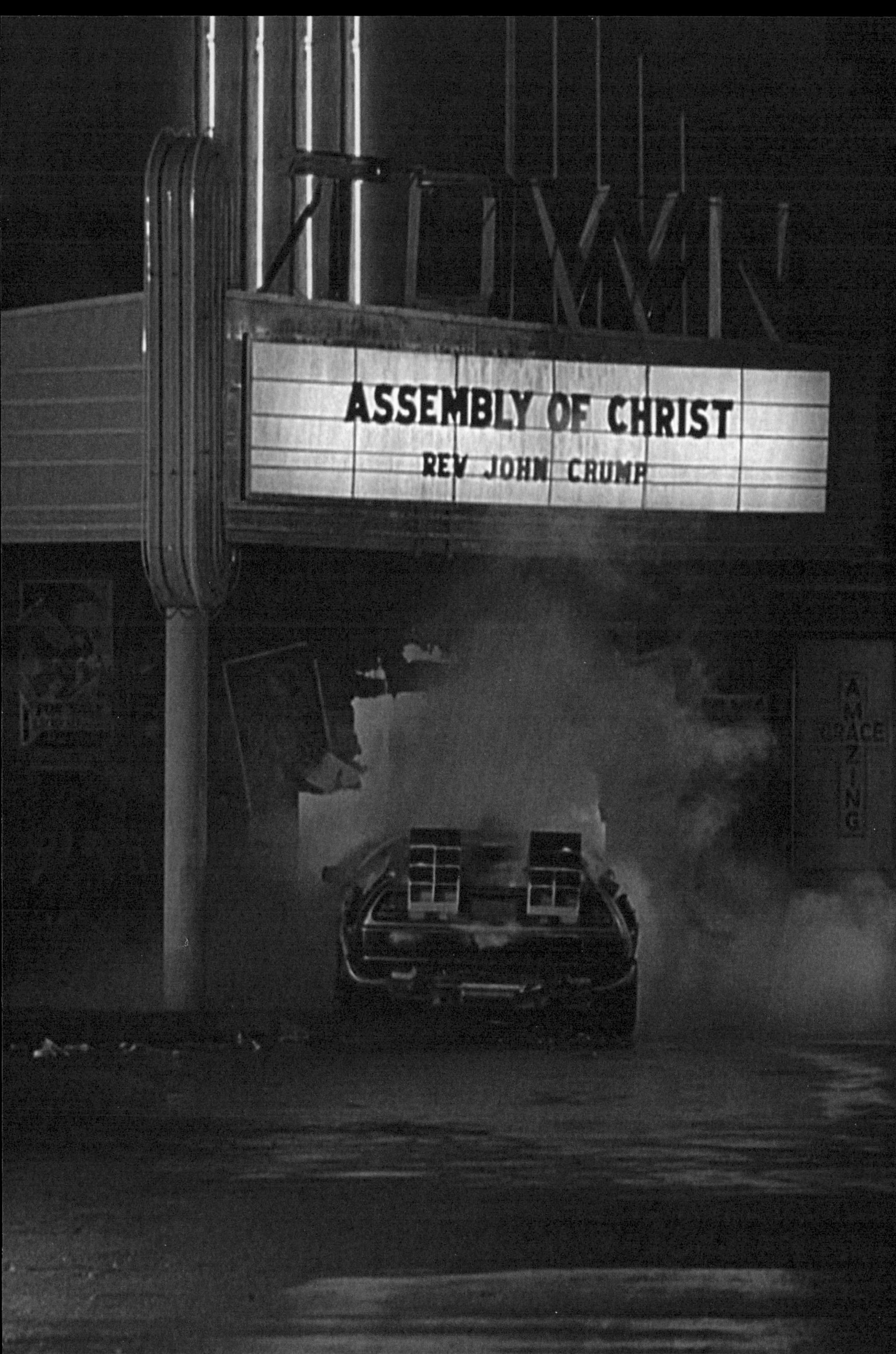
ASSEMBLY OF CHRIST
REV JOHN CRUMP
AMAZING GRACE

1985

The thrilling, time-traveling adventure of *Back to the Future* starts in good ol' 1985—and so do we. Picture 1985: Ronald Reagan is president, Huey Lewis is all over the airwaves, the Cola Wars are intensifying, hair is bigger, and life is more fast-paced than ever. This is the decade that brought us convenience food to be cooked in minutes in the microwave or enjoyed in the fluorescent ambience of a 7-Eleven. While the recipes in this chapter require a little more effort than the push of a button, they're largely quick and easy—perfect for a busy scientist or a skateboarding teenager running late for school.

LATE FOR SCHOOL PUFF-PASTRY TOASTER TARTS

Between school, homework, band practice, time with your friends, and regular visits with your friendly neighborhood scientist, it's sometimes hard to remember to eat breakfast. Luckily, in 1985, the frozen toaster pastry was invented—the perfect meal to eat one-handed while riding a skateboard to school. Wrap up a couple of these and store them in the freezer for those days when unexplained events necessitate breakfast on the go.

TIP:
ONCE BAKED, THESE WILL KEEP IN THE FREEZER UP TO 1 MONTH. SKIP THE ICING, WRAP EACH TART IN PARCHMENT PAPER, AND FREEZE. TO REHEAT, SIMPLY POP FROZEN TARTS IN THE TOASTER OVEN AT 400°F FOR 5 MINUTES.

YIELD: 6 PASTRIES

FOR THE TARTS:

1 tablespoon cornstarch, divided

⅔ cup strawberry jam

⅔ cup creamy peanut butter

2 sheets puff pastry, thawed

1 large egg

1 tablespoon cold water

FOR THE ICING:

2 tablespoons salted butter, melted

1½ cups powdered sugar

2 tablespoons half-and-half, plus more if needed

½ teaspoon vanilla extract

1. Preheat the oven to 425°F. Line a baking sheet or cookie sheet with parchment paper and set aside.

2. To make the tarts: Divide the cornstarch between 2 medium bowls. Mix the jam into one, the peanut butter into the other. Unfold a sheet of puff pastry, and cut into 6 equal rectangles. Transfer rectangles to the prepared baking sheet. Divide the peanut butter mixture evenly between the pieces, and spread it out, stopping half an inch from the edges. Spread the jam over the peanut butter.

3. In a small bowl, whisk the egg with the water to make an egg wash. Unfold the second sheet of puff pastry and cut it into 6 rectangles, then brush them lightly with egg wash. Place on top of the peanut butter and jelly pastry, egg wash side down, and use a fork to crimp the edges. Brush the tops with egg wash, and bake until golden brown, about 20 minutes.

4. To make the icing: Whisk all the ingredients until smooth. If the icing is too thick, whisk in a bit more half-and-half, ½ teaspoon at a time, until the icing can be drizzled over the pastries. Let pastries cool at least 5 minutes before icing.

THE PINHEADS' POST-PRACTICE CEREAL TREATS

There are only two acceptable ways to play rock and roll: loud and louder. A few hours of high-volume band practice can (literally) blow you away, but these sweet treats give a teenage guitarist a sweet pick-me-up that will have him back to shredding faster than Eddie Van Halen.

YIELD: 24 CEREAL TREATS

5 tablespoons unsalted butter, softened

One 10-ounce bag mini marshmallows

½ teaspoon kosher salt

1 teaspoon vanilla extract

3 cups crispy rice cereal

3 cups square multigrain cereal

¾ cup candy-coated peanut butter chocolate pieces

¾ cup candy-coated chocolate pieces

1. Grease a 9-by-13-inch baking dish with 1 tablespoon of the butter, and set aside.

2. Melt the remaining butter in a large saucepan on medium heat. Once butter is melted, add the entire bag of mini marshmallows and cook, stirring, until marshmallows are completely melted, about 2 minutes. Remove the pan from the heat, stir in the salt and vanilla, then add the cereals, and stir until fully coated. Stir in the candy pieces.

3. Pour the cereal mix into the prepared baking dish. Wet your hands with cold water, shake off any excess, and press the cereal mix evenly into the pan. Press a sheet of plastic wrap directly on top of the cereal treats, then let cool completely, and cut into squares for serving.

BATTLE OF THE BANDS COLA CAKE

Hill Valley High students and teachers didn't understand Calvin Klein's music in 1955, and 30 years later, they still thought it was "too darn loud." If you feel like you'll never amount to anything, just remember, cake usually has a way of making you feel better.

YIELD: 12 SERVINGS

FOR THE CAKE:

Cooking spray or butter, for pan

2 cups all-purpose flour

1 cup sugar

1 cup light brown sugar

1 teaspoon baking soda

3 tablespoons unsweetened cocoa powder

2 eggs

½ teaspoon kosher salt

1 cup unsalted butter, melted

1 cup cola

½ cup buttermilk

1 teaspoon vanilla extract

FOR THE FROSTING:

½ cup butter

⅓ cup cola

4 cups powdered sugar

3 tablespoons Dutch-process cocoa powder

2 tablespoons peanut butter

1 cup chopped peanuts

1. Preheat the oven to 350°F. Grease a 9-by-13-inch baking dish with cooking spray or butter, and set aside.

2. To make the cake: In a large bowl, combine the flour, sugar, brown sugar, baking soda, and cocoa powder. Make a well in the center of the dry ingredients, pour in the eggs, salt, and melted butter, and beat together with a fork. Beat in the cola, buttermilk, and vanilla until smooth, then stir the dry ingredients into the wet ingredients until just combined.

3. Pour the batter into the baking dish, using a spatula to spread it out evenly. Bake 35 to 40 minutes, until a wooden toothpick inserted into the center of the cake comes out clean. Let cool completely.

4. To make the frosting: Combine the butter and cola in a medium saucepan on medium heat, and bring to a boil. Transfer to a stand mixer, and add the powdered sugar, cocoa powder, and peanut butter. Beat on high speed until fluffy. Spread the frosting over the top of the cake, and cover with chopped peanuts before serving.

NEEDLES' NACHOS

Leave it to a gang of truck-racing goons to be masters of convenience store cuisine.

YIELD: 1 LARGE PLATTER (5 TO 10 SERVINGS)

One 1.25-ounce package taco seasoning

Two 15-ounce cans beef chili without beans

One 9-ounce can bean dip

1 cup sour cream

One 12-ounce bag tortilla chips

One 11-ounce bag corn chips

One 15-ounce jar queso blanco

One 15-ounce jar nacho cheese

½ cup jarred jalapeños, drained

One 6½-ounce can sliced black olives, drained

½ cup peperoncini, drained

¼ cup diced white onion

1 Roma tomato, diced

¼ cup fresh cilantro, chopped

1. Line a baking sheet with foil, and set aside.

2. In a small saucepan on medium heat, combine taco seasoning and chili, and heat until warm. In a small bowl, combine the bean dip and 2 ounces of the sour cream to thin it out.

3. Spread half the tortilla chips and corn chips onto the pan in a single layer. Heat up the queso blanco and nacho cheese and drizzle over tortilla chips. Pour half the chili, followed by half the beans, over the tortilla chips, and sprinkle half the jalapeños, black olives, and peperoncini on top. Repeat with another layer of tortilla chips and corn chips, and top with the remaining cheese, chili, and beans. Garnish with remaining jalapeños, black olives, peperoncini, onion, tomato, sour cream, and cilantro, and serve.

JENNIFER'S LAKESIDE CAMPING TRAIL MIX

Bring a bag of this to munch on during your long drive up to the lake, or to snack on as you cuddle with your high school sweetheart while gazing up at the stars.

YIELD: 12 CUPS

3 tablespoons light corn syrup

½ cup unsalted butter

¾ cup firmly packed light brown sugar

½ teaspoon kosher salt

½ teaspoon baking soda

1 teaspoon vanilla extract

4 cups cone-shaped fried corn snacks

4 cups crispy rice cereal squares

1 cup small salted pretzel twists

1 cup walnut halves, toasted

1½ cups (10 ounces) candy-coated chocolate pieces

1. Preheat the oven to 375°F. Line a baking sheet with foil, and set aside.

2. In a small saucepan on medium heat, combine the corn syrup, butter, brown sugar, and salt, and bring to a simmer. Cook, stirring occasionally until the sugar dissolves, about 3 to 5 minutes. Remove from heat; stir in the baking soda and vanilla.

3. In a large bowl, toss the corn snacks, rice cereal, pretzel twists, and walnut halves. Add the syrup, and stir well. Spread the mixture onto the pan, and bake 20 minutes, stirring every 5 minutes. Let cool completely, then toss with the candy-coated chocolate pieces. Pour trail mix into a resealable bag for an easy snack on the go.

McFLY FAMILY TABLE
TUNA NOODLE CASSEROLE

This casserole classic is a full meal in one dish, so you can spend less time focusing on dinner and more time enjoying your favorite old sitcom with the family.

YIELD: 8 SERVINGS

One 16-ounce package wide egg noodles

Two 10.5-ounce cans cream of mushroom soup

1 cup milk

Two 10-ounce cans white albacore tuna in water, drained

3 cups frozen vegetable medley

¼ cup crushed buttery cracker crumbs

2 tablespoons unsalted butter, melted

1. Preheat the oven to 375°F.

2. Boil the egg noodles in a large pot of salted water until just cooked, then drain well and pour back into the pot. Stir in the soup, milk, tuna, and frozen vegetables, then pour into a 9-by-13-inch casserole dish, and bake 40 minutes, stirring occasionally.

3. In a small bowl, combine the crushed crackers and melted butter. Sprinkle over the casserole, then bake another 5 to 10 minutes until golden and crispy. Serve hot.

UNCLE JOEY'S PAROLE CAKE

It's a mystery whether Uncle Joey's actually going to make parole. Let's hope he does so we can celebrate with a custom-themed cake.

YIELD: 12 SERVINGS

FOR THE CAKE:

Butter or cooking spray, to grease the pan

3½ cups all-purpose flour

1 tablespoon baking powder

1 tablespoon baking soda

1 tablespoon kosher salt

4 cups sugar

4 large eggs

1 cup milk

1 cup buttermilk

1 cup vegetable oil

1½ tablespoons vanilla extract

1½ cups unsweetened cocoa powder

2 cups boiling water

FOR THE FROSTING:

1 cup unsalted butter, softened

4 cups powdered sugar

¼ cup milk

1 tablespoon vanilla extract

Red, black, and blue food coloring

1. Preheat the oven to 350°F. Lightly grease a 9-by-13-inch baking dish with butter or cooking spray, line with parchment paper, and set aside.

2. To make the cake: Sift together the flour, baking powder, baking soda, and salt into a large bowl. Whisk in the sugar, eggs, milk, buttermilk, oil, and vanilla until smooth. In a separate medium bowl or measuring cup, stir together the cocoa powder and boiling water, then whisk into the batter until just combined.

3. Pour the batter into the baking dish, and bake 35 to 40 minutes or until a wooden skewer inserted into the center comes out clean. Let cool completely before frosting.

4. To make the frosting: In a medium bowl, using a hand mixer set to low speed, cream the butter, powdered sugar, milk, and vanilla until combined. Raise speed to medium-high, and beat until light and fluffy, 5 to 7 minutes.

5. Divide the frosting in half, and then divide one half among 3 small bowls. Add food coloring so you have a bowl each of red, black, and blue frosting. Scoop frosting into 3 piping bags fitted with small tips.

TO ASSEMBLE:

6. Cover the top of the cake with the remaining vanilla frosting. Pipe "Welcome Home Uncle Joey" in red frosting along the top and bottom of the cake.

7. Use black frosting to pipe a flying bird on the right side of the cake and an open jail cell on the left. Use the blue frosting to fill in the open jail cell door, as well as the beak and feet of the bird. (See image for reference.)

8. Slice and serve.

PLUTONIUM PESTO PASTA SALAD

This delectable pesto pasta is not exactly weapons-grade, but it tastes so good you won't believe it's legal.

YIELD: 8 TO 10 SERVINGS

4 cups chopped fresh basil leaves

6 cloves garlic

1 cup shredded Parmesan

½ cup toasted pecans

1 teaspoon kosher salt

1 tablespoon red pepper flakes

⅛ cup freshly squeezed lemon juice

⅓ cup fresh flat-leaf parsley

¾ cup olive oil

2 pounds ziti

½ cup mascarpone

1 pint grape tomatoes, halved

1 pound fresh mozzarella, cubed

1. In a food processor, pulse the basil, garlic, Parmesan, pecans, salt, red pepper, lemon juice, parsley, and olive oil until combined, scraping down the sides of the bowl a few times to ensure a smooth pesto.

2. Bring a large pot of salted water to a boil. Cook the ziti until al dente, about 10 minutes, then drain. Toss the hot ziti with the mascarpone and pesto. Once the pasta is fully coated, stir in the grape tomatoes and mozzarella cubes. Serve family style in a big pasta bowl.

FROZEN-IN-TIME PUDDING POPS

Countless American freezers in 1985 contained at least one box of pudding pops. If you've ever pined for those long-discontinued tasty frozen treats, don't despair—with this recipe, you've got the power to recreate them. It's like going back in time right in your own kitchen!

YIELD: 12 TO 16 POPS

5½ cups milk

1 cup sugar

6 tablespoons unsweetened cocoa powder

¼ teaspoon kosher salt

½ cup cornstarch

4 tablespoons unsalted butter

1 tablespoon vanilla extract

SPECIAL SUPPLIES:
Reusable ice-pop molds

1. In a large heavy-bottom saucepan on medium-high heat, combine the milk, sugar, cocoa powder, salt, and cornstarch. Cook, whisking constantly, until the mixture comes to a boil and thickens to a pudding-like consistency, 4 to 5 minutes. Remove from heat, and whisk in butter and vanilla. Pour the mixture into a bowl, cover with plastic wrap, and let cool completely. Once cool, pour into ice-pop molds, and freeze 5 hours or until solid.

1955

Greetings from the nifty '50s! This is the decade when families would gather around the table each night for dinners that would come to define comfort food, like pot roast, meat loaf, and chicken pot pie. It's the decade of carhops and doo-wop, of soda jerks slinging egg creams and lime rickeys, of drive-in movie theaters and burger joints. The meals you're about to enjoy are a true time-travel experience, adapted from some of the most popular recipes of the decade, and cooked with love by every happy housewife in Hill Valley.

Mr. Peabody's Pignoli Cookies

The residents of Hill Valley never understood Old Man Peabody's obsession with pine trees—maybe because they never got to try his delicious, gluten-free, pine-nut-based cookies. If they had, they might have been more inclined to save his ranch instead of letting developers turn it into the Twin Pines Mall.

Yield: About 24 cookies ....

Butter, for pan

12 ounces almond paste

½ cup sugar

4 egg whites

1 cup powdered sugar

2 tablespoons cold water

1½ cups pine nuts

1. Preheat the oven to 325°F. Line 2 cookie sheets with foil, lightly grease the foil with butter, and set aside.

2. In a food processor, pulse the almond paste and sugar until smooth. Add 2 of the egg whites and the powdered sugar, and continue pulsing until a soft dough forms.

3. In a small bowl, whisk the remaining 2 egg whites with the water. Roughly chop the pine nuts, and put them on a plate. With lightly floured hands, roll almond dough into 1-inch balls. Coat balls in egg wash, shaking off excess, then roll in pine nuts, pressing lightly to ensure that the nuts stick to the dough. Place the balls on the cookie sheet at least 2 inches apart. Bake 15 to 18 minutes, or until lightly brown, then transfer to a wire rack to cool completely before serving.

Mr. Caruthers's Egg Cream

The most iconic drink at the soda fountain is the egg cream, and you can bet your bottom dollar the one Lou Caruthers pours at his café located in Courthouse Square is the bee's knees.

Yield: 1 egg cream ....

¾ cup cold milk

3 tablespoons chocolate syrup

¾ cup cold seltzer

1. In a pint glass, stir together the milk and chocolate syrup. While stirring briskly, slowly pour in the seltzer, stopping when the egg cream has developed a big, foamy head. Insert a straw and serve immediately.

Mrs. Baines's Meat Loaf

Sometimes you end up with a surprise guest at the dinner table, like when an old friend stops by to say hello, or your husband accidentally hits a teenage boy with his car. If you're looking to stretch a meal to feed a crowd, you can't go wrong with a moist, hearty meat loaf.

Yield: 8 to 10 servings

½ cup grated carrot

½ cup grated onion

½ cup diced celery

2 tablespoons olive oil

1 pound ground beef

1 pound ground pork

3 cups panko bread crumbs

2 eggs, well beaten

1 tablespoon kosher salt

2 teaspoons black pepper

1 teaspoon paprika

One 10.5-ounce can cream of mushroom soup

6 strips bacon

1 cup ketchup

¼ cup light brown sugar

1 tablespoon Worcestershire sauce

1. Preheat the oven to 375°F. Line a roasting pan with foil, then place a roasting rack inside.

2. In a large skillet on medium-high heat, sauté the carrot, onion, and celery in olive oil until soft, about 5 minutes. In a large bowl, combine the sautéed vegetables with the beef, pork, panko, eggs, salt, pepper, paprika, and soup. Form the mixture into a compact loaf shape, then place on the roasting rack and wrap in the bacon. Bake 30 minutes.

3. In a small bowl, whisk together the ketchup, light brown sugar, and Worcestershire sauce. Brush onto the meat loaf, and continue cooking, brushing with extra glaze every 10 minutes or so, until a thermometer inserted into the center of the meat loaf registers 160°F. Let rest 10 minutes, transfer to a platter, and serve.

Goldie Wilson Mayoral Tuna Melt

Many Hill Valley citizens cast their vote for Mayor Goldie Wilson because they remembered his days of friendly service at Lou's Cafe, where his attention to detail and can-do attitude could make even a simple tuna melt feel like a four-star meal. That sort of commitment to excellence is exactly what city hall needs.

Yield: 4 sandwiches

8 slices white, whole wheat, or rye bread

Two 10-ounce cans white albacore tuna in water, drained

¾ cup mayonnaise

1 teaspoon kosher salt

½ teaspoon black pepper

2 small ribs celery, minced

½ teaspoon garlic powder

½ teaspoon paprika

½ cup panko bread crumbs

16 slices Swiss, pepper jack, or American cheese

1. Preheat the oven to 400°F. Place the bread on a baking sheet, and toast 7 to 10 minutes or until golden.

2. In a medium bowl, combine the tuna, mayonnaise, salt, pepper, celery, garlic powder, paprika, and panko. Taste for seasoning, adjusting as desired. Divide among the toast, then top each with 2 slices of cheese, and bake 10 to 15 minutes, or until the cheese is brown and bubbly. Serve immediately.

Essex Theater Lime Rickey

Once upon a time, movie snacks were more than just sodas and popcorn. Back in 1955, many small-town theaters, like Hill Valley's Essex, had snack bars with a full soda fountain, where a soda jerk could whip you up a cool lime rickey to sip while enjoying the latest double feature. Next time you park yourself on the couch for an at-home movie marathon, set up your own refreshment bar with all the ingredients needed to make this refreshing retro cooler.

Yield: 2 cups lime syrup or 16 lime rickeys

FOR THE LIME SYRUP:

1 cup sugar

1 cup freshly squeezed lime juice, from about 8 limes

Zest of 6 limes

FOR THE RICKEY:

Seltzer water, to fill the glass

1 tablespoon cherry syrup

Maraschino cherries, for garnishing

TO MAKE THE LIME SYRUP:

1. In a small saucepan on medium heat, combine the sugar and lime juice, and bring to a boil. Reduce the heat to low, and stir in the lime zest. Cook 5 minutes, strain the syrup into a glass measuring cup, and cool completely.

TO MAKE THE RICKEY:

2. Fill a pint glass halfway with ice. Pour 2 tablespoons of lime syrup into the glass, and fill the rest of the glass with seltzer. Stir, then top with a tablespoon of cherry syrup and a maraschino cherry. Insert straw, and serve.

Holt's Diner Chocolate Malted Milkshake

After taking his best girl to see *The Atomic Kid* at the Town Theater, a teenager in love could keep the date going by heading next door to Holt's Diner for a late-night chocolate malted milkshake—the best in Hill Valley!

Yield: 2 milkshakes

1 pint chocolate ice cream

⅓ cup malted milk powder

1 cup milk, plus more as needed

Whipped cream, for garnish

1. In a blender, combine the chocolate ice cream and malted milk powder. Add 1 cup of milk, and blend on low until smooth, about 1 minute. Add more milk as needed until you reach the desired thickness of your shake.

2. Divide shake between 2 glasses, garnish with whipped cream, and serve.

Biff's Corned Beef Hash Skillet

Biff can't hang out with the boys on Sunday until he's done with his homework. A hearty skillet of corned beef hash and eggs should give him plenty of energy to sit down and get to work copying George's answers in his own handwriting.

Yield: 4 servings

4 tablespoons butter

2 yellow onions, diced

Salt and pepper

3 large russet potatoes, baked and cut into chunks

½ pound corned beef, sliced thin and roughly chopped

¼ cup chicken stock

4 eggs

Hot sauce, for serving

1. Melt the butter in a cast iron skillet on high heat. Add the onion, season with salt and pepper to taste, and cook until translucent, about 3 minutes. Add the baked potatoes to the skillet, and fry until they begin to brown, 5 to 7 minutes. Add the corned beef to the skillet, along with the chicken stock. Stir everything together, then spread the hash to cover the bottom of the skillet.

2. Cook the hash without touching it for 5 to 8 minutes, until a crispy brown crust forms on the bottom. While the hash is cooking, preheat the broiler on high. Flip the hash (it's okay if it breaks up), then crack the eggs directly on top. Remove the skillet from the stove and slide it under the broiler. Cook until the eggs are done to your liking, about 3 to 5 minutes. Serve with plenty of hot sauce.

George McFly's Blob From Outer Space

Even before his encounter with Darth Vader from planet Vulcan, George McFly was a true believer in the existence of extraterrestrials. This jiggly gelatin blob looks like it could have starred in one of his favorite sci-fi B movies. Serve it just as the recipe states, or use inventive garnishes such as marshmallows or gummy fish to make an out-of-this-world creature all your own.

Yield: 4 to 6 servings

One 3-ounce box lime gelatin

1 cup boiling water

1 cup cold water

One 40-ounce can sliced pineapple, drained (reserve the can)

8 maraschino cherries

OPTIONAL GARNISHES:

Sliced fruit

Mini marshmallows

Gummy fish, licorice vines, or other movie candies

1. In a large liquid measuring cup, stir the lime gelatin into the boiling water until dissolved, then add the cold water. Set aside.

2. Place 1 pineapple ring into the empty can, insert a maraschino cherry into its center, then pour in just enough lime gelatin to cover. Repeat the process until the can is full, then cover with plastic and refrigerate at least 4 hours. (There will be gelatin left over—discard, or pour into a small bowl and refrigerate.)

TO UNMOLD:

3. Run the outside of the can under hot tap water for 30 seconds, then invert, open end down, onto a plate. Remove the top with a can opener, then unmold. Serve as is or slice the rings individually.

Pohatchee Drive-In Cheeseburgers

There's nothing like a classic drive-in cheeseburger, but this one is infused with a distinctive smoky, spicy sauce in honor of the Western theme of the Pohatchee Drive-In.

Yield: 4 burgers ....

FOR THE SAUCE:

4 tablespoons mayonnaise

2 tablespoons ketchup

4 tablespoons barbecue sauce

1 to 2 teaspoons hot sauce (to taste)

1 tablespoon honey

TO MAKE THE SAUCE:

1. In a small bowl, whisk together the mayonnaise, ketchup, barbecue sauce, hot sauce, and honey. Set aside.

FOR THE BURGERS:

1 pound ground beef (70% lean, 30% fat)

2 tablespoons unsalted butter

Salt and pepper

4 slices American cheese

4 hamburger buns

¼ head iceberg lettuce, shredded

Dill pickle chips

1 Roma tomato, sliced

One small white onion, diced

TO MAKE THE BURGERS:

2. Split the ground beef into 8 equal portions, roll into balls, and flatten. Preheat a cast iron skillet on high. When the skillet is hot, add the butter and melt. Working in batches if necessary, add beef patties and smash flat with the back of a spatula, then salt and pepper generously, and cook until the edges of the burgers become brown and crispy—2 to 3 minutes. Flip, sprinkle with a bit more salt and pepper, then top each patty with a cheese slice, and cook another 2 minutes.

3. Split the hamburger buns, spreading sauce on each half. Add shredded lettuce to the bottom buns, then top each with 2 patties. Add pickles, tomatoes, onion, and the top bun, and serve.

Rerun Spaghetti With Meat Sauce

After traveling through the space-time continuum, a big bowl of spaghetti is just the thing to make you feel right at home. In fact, why not make some extra to have leftovers for tomorrow, so you can spend less time in the kitchen and more time enjoying the next episode of *The Honeymooners*.

Yield: 8 servings

3 tablespoons olive oil

1 pound ground beef

½ pound Italian sausage, removed from casing

2 teaspoons kosher salt

1 teaspoon black pepper

1 large onion, diced

2 carrots, grated

6 large cloves garlic, minced

2 tablespoons tomato paste

1 teaspoon red pepper flakes

Two 28-ounce cans crushed tomatoes

2 teaspoons dried parsley

1 teaspoon dried oregano

1 teaspoon dried basil

2 pounds spaghetti, cooked al dente

½ cup grated Parmesan

1. Heat olive oil in a large saucepan or Dutch oven on high. Add the beef and sausage, and season with salt and pepper. Cook, breaking the meat up with a wooden spoon, for 5 minutes or until deeply brown. Transfer meat into a strainer set over a large bowl, reserving some of the drippings in the pan.

2. Return the pan to the heat, and add the onion and carrot. Cook until onion is translucent, 3 to 5 minutes, then stir in the garlic and cook another minute or so, until fragrant. Stir in the tomato paste and cook, stirring occasionally, another 2 to 3 minutes, until the mixture begins to caramelize. Add the red pepper and cook another 30 seconds.

3. Pour in the tomatoes, add the dried herbs, stir well, then add the meat back to the pot. Bring the sauce to a boil, then reduce to a simmer, and cook 1 hour, stirring frequently. Taste for seasoning, adding more salt, pepper, and herbs as you like.

4. Toss the meat sauce and spaghetti together in a large bowl, top with Parmesan, and serve. Store the leftovers in a casserole dish for tomorrow's "rerun," when you'll reheat it in the microwave or a 350°F oven.

Mr. Strickland's Newspaper-Wrapped Red Snapper

While a slacker might just toss a snapper directly on the grill, a smart, respectable citizen like Mr. Strickland knows that wrapping the whole fish in wet newspaper before grilling it will trap the moisture inside, resulting in a delicious, tender meal. Be like Mr. Strickland and you'll never have to settle for a subpar snapper.

Yield: 2 servings

1 whole red snapper, cleaned and descaled (ask your fishmonger)

Salt and pepper

2 large lemons, thinly sliced

¼ cup freshly squeezed lemon juice

¼ cup olive oil

1 clove garlic, grated or finely minced

½ cup fresh flat-leaf parsley, chopped

2 tablespoons finely minced shallots

SPECIAL SUPPLIES:

5 sheets newspaper

1 sheet parchment paper

1. Preheat the grill. If using a gas grill, turn the burners on one side to high. If using charcoal, push all the coals to one side. Slightly dampen the newspaper under running water.

2. Season the inside of the snapper with salt and pepper, and place a few slices of lemon into the cavity. Lay some lemon slices in the middle of the parchment paper. Place the snapper on top of them, then cover with the remaining lemon slices. Wrap the fish in the parchment paper, then wrap tightly in newspaper. Place the wrapped fish on the grill over indirect heat, close the lid, and cook 30 minutes, flipping over halfway through.

3. In a small bowl, whisk together the lemon juice, olive oil, garlic, parsley, and shallots. Season with salt and pepper, to taste. Let sit at least 15 minutes.

4. Unwrap the snapper, move to a platter, and discard the lemon slices. Serve immediately with the sauce on the side.

Doc Brown's Time-Altering Chicken Pot Pie

Great Scott! Falling and hitting your head on a toilet isn't usually a reason to celebrate, but if it leads to an invention that can, quite literally, change history like the Flux Capacitor, one way to mark the occasion is with a special dinner. Copernicus will be happy to lick the plate clean.

Yield: 4 to 6 servings ....

4 tablespoons butter

1 pound boneless, skinless chicken breasts or thighs, cut into large chunks

1 medium onion, diced

2 carrots, diced

Salt

⅓ cup all-purpose flour

1¾ cups chicken broth

⅔ cup evaporated milk

½ cup frozen peas, thawed

½ teaspoon chopped flat-leaf parsley

Black pepper

1 egg

1 tablespoon water

1 package ready-to-use refrigerated pie dough (2 sheets)

1. Preheat the oven to 425°F.

2. In a large skillet on high heat, melt 2 tablespoons of the butter. Add the chicken to the skillet, working in batches if necessary, and cook until brown on all sides, about 7 to 10 minutes. Remove to a plate, and set aside.

3. Add the onion and carrot to the pan with the remaining butter and a pinch of salt, and cook, stirring occasionally, until softened, 3 to 5 minutes. Stir the flour into the veggies, until no raw specks are visible. Add the chicken broth and evaporated milk, stir to combine, and bring to a boil. Add the chicken, reduce the heat to low, and simmer 5 minutes. Stir in the peas and parsley, taste for seasoning, and add more salt and pepper as desired.

4. In a small bowl, beat together the egg and 1 tablespoon of water to make an egg wash. Pour the filling into a pie pan, and cover with 1 sheet of dough, pressing the edges to seal. Brush with egg wash.

5. Place the second sheet of dough on a lightly floured surface. Using a sharp paring knife, cut out the Y-like symbol of the flux capacitor. Place your flux capacitor on the center of your pie, and brush with egg wash. Use cookie cutters or a knife to cut the numbers 1 to 12 from the remaining scraps of dough, rerolling if necessary, then arrange them around the circumference of the pie like a clock face, and brush with egg wash. Cut a few small vent holes in the dough to let steam escape.

6. Bake 25 to 30 minutes, until golden brown. Let cool 10 minutes before serving.

The Starlighters' Baked Alaska

It ain't nobody's business what the band is doing in their car while on break. Just know that if you're looking for a heavy duty lighter to toast your meringue, they might be able to help.

Yield: 6 to 10 servings

1 loaf pound cake

½ gallon Neapolitan ice cream

7 egg whites

Pinch cream of tartar

⅔ cup sugar

SPECIAL SUPPLIES:

Kitchen torch (or broiler)

1. Cut the pound cake into 1-inch slices. Line the bottom of a 9-inch pie pan with the pieces, cutting them to fit as needed. Scoop the ice cream on top, cover with plastic wrap, and use your hands to shape it into a dome. Freeze at least 2 hours, until solid.

2. Combine the egg whites and cream of tartar in a medium bowl, and beat with a hand mixer set to medium speed until foamy. Continue beating while slowly streaming in the sugar, then whip until the meringue forms stiff peaks.

3. Remove the ice cream cake from freezer. Using a spatula, gently spread the meringue over the ice cream. Use a kitchen torch to brown the outside, or put it under the broiler, approximately 6 inches from the flame, for a few minutes (do not take your eye off it!) until the meringue is toasted. Serve immediately.

Marvin (Straw) Berry Sundae

Call your cousin Chuck, because it looks like you've stumbled upon that dessert he's looking for.

Yield: 2 sundaes ....

1 pint strawberries

½ cup sugar

½ teaspoon kosher salt

1 teaspoon vanilla extract

12 shortbread cookies

1 pint vanilla ice cream

Whipped cream, for garnish

2 maraschino cherries

1. Quarter the strawberries, and place in a medium bowl. Add sugar, salt, and vanilla. Stir well to dissolve the sugar, and let sit 30 minutes.

2. Place the shortbread cookies into a resealable bag and use a rolling pin to roughly break them up. Divide half the shortbread crumbs between 2 bowls. Add 2 scoops of ice cream to each bowl and top with ½ cup of the strawberries and their juices. Garnish with whipped cream, sprinkle with remaining shortbread crumbs, top with a maraschino cherry, and serve immediately.

Enchantment Under the Sea Punch

This classic tropical punch gets an extra dose of enchantment when you make it Biff's way. Just make sure your guests know it's spiked before serving. Who knows? It might even give you the courage to kiss the girl of your dreams.

Yield: 10+ servings

One 2-liter bottle ginger ale

One 2-liter bottle lemon-lime soda

Two 12-ounce cans pineapple juice

One 750-ml bottle vodka (optional)

One 16-ounce container rainbow sherbet

One 32-ounce bag frozen pineapple chunks

2 navel oranges, sliced thin

1. In a large punch bowl, stir together the ginger ale, lemon-lime soda, pineapple juice, and vodka (if using). Scoop the sherbet into the center of the bowl, then add the frozen pineapple and orange slices. Serve immediately.

2015

Ah, 2015: the far future. At least it was in 1989 when *Back to the Future Part II* sent Marty and Doc thirty years forward to a time of hoverboards, flying cars, holographic advertisements, and tech-enhanced fashion. The real 2015 may not have looked all that much like the filmmakers imagined, but with some culinary craftiness and a little of imagination, you can still experience their particular radical retrofuturism in the kitchen.

EXPLODING CANDY TOASTER TARTS

They say history repeats itself, and Marty Jr. is, after all, the spitting image of his dear old dad. Marty typically starts his mornings with hot Late for School Puff-Pastry Toaster Tarts (page 17), and Marty Jr. is not much different—though the breakfast pastries of the future certainly have changed.

YIELD: 6 PASTRIES

FOR THE FILLING:

4 tablespoons butter

1½ cups semisweet chocolate chips

1 cup heavy cream

FOR THE TARTS:

1 egg

1 tablespoon water

1 package ready-to-use refrigerated pie dough (2 sheets)

FOR THE ROYAL ICING:

1 egg white

¼ teaspoon white vinegar

2 cups powdered sugar

Food coloring of choice (optional)

2 packets exploding candy of choice, for topping

1. To make the filling: Combine butter and chocolate chips in a large bowl. In a small saucepan on medium-high heat, bring the heavy cream almost to a boil. Pour the cream over the chocolate and butter, and let sit 1 minute. Stir well, until the chocolate filling is smooth, then set aside 5 minutes to cool and thicken slightly.

2. To make the tarts: In a small bowl, beat the egg with the water to make an egg wash. Unroll the dough, cut each sheet into sixths, and brush with egg wash. Divide the chocolate filling between 6 of the pieces, spreading it to ½ inch from the edge, then top with the remaining pastry pieces, egg wash side down. (You may need to stretch these a little to make them fit.) Crimp the edges with a fork to seal, then freeze at least 20 minutes or until firm. Cover the egg wash with plastic wrap, and store it in the refrigerator.

3. Preheat the oven to 350°F. Remove the tarts from the freezer. Brush the tops with the remaining egg wash, and bake 25 to 30 minutes or until golden brown.

4. To make the royal icing: In a medium bowl, using a hand mixer set to medium speed, whisk the egg white and vinegar until foamy. Whisk in the powdered sugar ¼ cup at a time until a thick icing forms. Add food coloring, if using, a drop at a time until you achieve the color you want.

5. Spread icing over pastries and sprinkle with exploding candies. (If the icing becomes too thick, whisk in some hot water, ½ teaspoon at a time, until it reaches your desired consistency.) Let the icing harden completely before serving, about 10 to 15 minutes.

THE SLEEP INDUCER

Hilldale is nothing but a breeding ground for tranks, lo-bos, and zipheads—probably better to enjoy an aperitif at home instead of going out on the town. Perhaps call some friends on the video TV, whip up a few Sleep Inducers, and have a virtual cocktail party in the comfort of your own den.

YIELD: 1 COCKTAIL

¼ cup coffee liqueur

¼ cup lemon-lime soda

¼ cup vodka

Lime twist, for garnish

1. Hold a spoon upside down over a small cordial glass filled with crushed ice. Float the coffee liqueur into the glass, followed by the lemon-lime soda, followed by the vodka. Garnish with a lime twist, and serve.

CAFÉ '80S BURRITO

Burritos taste b-b-b-better when they're served by d-d-d-digital celebrities. Make them to order with steak, chicken, or pork. No matter what filling you choose or which decade they're served in, these burritos are d-d-d-delicious.

YIELD: 4 BURRITOS

1 cup diced tomatoes

½ cup diced white onion

1 jalapeño, diced

Salt and black pepper

¼ cup plus 3 tablespoons freshly squeezed lime juice

16 ounces sour cream

1 chipotle pepper in adobo sauce, diced

2 tablespoons vegetable oil

1 pound fajita steak, pork, or chicken

2 teaspoons chile powder

2 cups cooked rice

¼ cup chopped fresh cilantro

4 large flour tortillas

8 ounces cotija cheese

1. In a small bowl, make the pico de gallo: Combine the tomatoes, onion, and jalapeño. Season with salt and pepper, toss with 1 tablespoon of the lime juice, and set aside. In a separate small bowl, combine the sour cream, chipotle, and 1 tablespoon of the lime juice, and set aside.

2. Heat a cast iron skillet on medium-high, then add the vegetable oil. Toss the fajita meat with the chile powder, add the meat to the skillet, and cook until brown, about 5 minutes. Add 1 tablespoon of lime juice to the skillet, and toss meat to ensure it's evenly coated. Remove from the skillet, and cover with a tented piece of aluminum foil to keep warm.

3. In a third small bowl, combine the rice, ¼ cup lime juice, and cilantro, and season with salt and pepper.

4. Heat the flour tortillas in the microwave or in a dry skillet until soft and pliable.

5. Spread the tortillas with the chipotle cream, then divide the rice, steak, and pico de gallo between them. Top with crumbled cotija, then roll up into burritos, and serve.

AUTO-ADJUSTING POPOVERS

Similar to your favorite self-drying, auto-fitting jacket that shrinks to size, popovers inflate in the oven with a hot burst of steam, then deflate once they're baked and ready to eat.

YIELD: 12 POPOVERS

3 eggs

1½ cups all-purpose flour

1½ cups milk

1½ teaspoons vanilla extract

½ teaspoon kosher salt

Cooking spray

Butter and jam or chocolate hazelnut spread, for serving

1. Pour the eggs, flour, milk, vanilla, and salt into a blender, and process 1 minute until smooth. Let batter sit at room temperature to hydrate while you preheat the oven to 450°F.

2. Grease a muffin pan with cooking spray, and divide the batter evenly between sections. Bake in the center of the oven 20 minutes, then reduce the heat to 350°F and bake another 15 to 20 minutes or until golden.

3. Serve immediately with butter and jam or hazelnut spread.

JAWS 19 SPICY GRILLED SHARK STEAKS

Surprising piece of movie trivia from 2015: In *Jaws 19*, the *humans* eat the *shark*. With these delicious grilled shark steaks on the menu, you're going to need a bigger plate.

YIELD: 4 SERVINGS

3 tablespoons sesame oil

2 teaspoons soy sauce

2 tablespoons gochujang

2 tablespoons Asian chili sauce

2 cloves garlic, minced

1 tablespoon freshly grated ginger

2 tablespoons honey

Four 6- to 9-ounce shark or swordfish steaks

Vegetable oil, for grill

1. In a medium bowl, whisk together the sesame oil, soy sauce, gochujang, chili sauce, garlic, ginger, and honey. Pour the marinade into a resealable container with the fish steaks, making sure they are coated completely, and refrigerate 2 to 4 hours. Let the marinated fish come to room temperature before cooking.

2. Preheat the grill to high. Dip a paper towel in vegetable oil and use it to rub down the grates, greasing them.

3. Grill the fish steaks 5 to 7 minutes per side, until the steaks reach an internal temperature of 145°F. Let rest 5 minutes, then serve.

MR. FUSION BANANA-FUELED PROTEIN BOWL

Who needs plutonium to get the day going when you can unleash the energy-producing power of healthy foods like bananas in your Mr. Fusion blender? If you don't happen to have a Mr. Fusion on hand, any alternative brand will do—fortunately this recipe does not require 1.21 gigawatts of power to come together.

YIELD: 1 SMOOTHIE

FOR THE SMOOTHIE:

1 cup almond milk

2 frozen bananas

¼ cup quick-cooking oats

3 tablespoons cashew butter

¼ teaspoon kosher salt

¼ teaspoon vanilla extract

2 tablespoons honey

FOR THE TOPPINGS:

Fresh banana slices

Toasted coconut

Fresh blueberries

Chia seeds

Chopped nuts

Chocolate chips

1. To make the smoothie: In a blender, combine the almond milk, bananas, oats, cashew butter, salt, vanilla, and honey. Puree 2 to 3 minutes until well combined, then pour into a bowl. Garnish with your choice of toppings, and serve immediately.

WHAT ARE YOU, CHICKEN? SANDWICH

What's the secret to kicking your fried-chicken sandwich up a notch? Spike the batter for your freshly fried thighs with hot sauce. That is, if you ain't too chicken.

YIELD: 4 SANDWICHES

4 boneless, skinless chicken thighs

2 cups buttermilk

3 teaspoons kosher salt, divided

1 cup flour

1 teaspoon cayenne pepper

1 teaspoon black pepper

1 cup plain panko bread crumbs

2 cups butter crackers, crushed

2 eggs

3 to 5 tablespoons hot sauce, divided

2 cups neutral oil, like canola or vegetable, for frying

¼ cup mayonnaise

2 tablespoons ketchup

1 tablespoon dill pickle juice

Dill pickle slices

4 potato buns, toasted

1. Place the chicken thighs between 2 pieces of plastic wrap, and, using a meat tenderizer, pound them to about ¼-inch thickness. Transfer the flattened chicken thighs to a resealable bag, and pour in the buttermilk and 2 teaspoons of the salt. Seal the bag, and refrigerate at least 4 hours or overnight.

2. On a plate, combine the flour, the remaining 1 teaspoon of salt, cayenne pepper, and black pepper. In a pie pan, combine the panko and cracker crumbs. Remove the chicken from the bag, and pour the buttermilk into another shallow pie pan. Add the eggs to the buttermilk with 1 to 2 tablespoons of hot sauce, depending on how spicy you like things, and beat until smooth.

3. In a large Dutch oven fitted with a deep-fry thermometer, heat the oil on high. When oil reaches 360 degrees, dredge chicken thighs in the flour, then the buttermilk mixture, then coat in the cracker crumbs, pressing well with your hands so the coating sticks. Gently lower the chicken into the hot oil, and fry 8 to 10 minutes, flipping once, until the chicken is golden on both sides.

4. In a small bowl, combine the mayonnaise, ketchup, 1 to 2 tablespoons hot sauce, and pickle juice. Spread sauce on each bun, and top with chicken and 1 to 2 dill pickle slices. Serve immediately.

HOVERBOARD COOKIES

You could go around the town square borrowing little kids' scooters and hoverboards, or you could bake these little beauties. They might not be much help in your chase sequence, but at least they look (and taste) like an absolute dream.

YIELD: ABOUT 3 DOZEN COOKIES

2 cups butter, softened

1 cup sugar

1 egg

1 teaspoon kosher salt

1 teaspoon vanilla extract

4 cups flour

2 cups white chocolate candy disks

Food coloring of choice

1. In the bowl of a stand mixer set to medium-high speed, cream the butter and sugar until light and fluffy. Beat in the egg, salt, and vanilla until combined. Add flour a little bit at a time, continuing to mix until everything is combined. Shape dough into a rectangle, wrap in plastic, and refrigerate 1 hour.

2. Preheat the oven to 350°F. Line a baking sheet with parchment paper, and set aside.

3. On a lightly floured surface, roll dough to ¼-inch thickness. Use a cookie cutter or a paring knife to cut 3-inch hoverboard shapes from the dough, and place on the baking sheet. Refrigerate 15 minutes, then transfer to the oven, and bake 10 to 13 minutes. Let cool on a wire rack.

4. In a microwave-safe bowl, heat the white chocolate candy disks in 30-second intervals until completely melted, stirring at each interval.

5. Divide white chocolate between small bowls and tint with food coloring of choice. Ice your hoverboards according to your own design but be quick—they might just float away.

TIP:
PINK, YELLOW, GREEN, AND WHITE ARE CLASSIC HOVERBOARD COLORS, BUT FEEL FREE TO GO ROGUE WITH YOUR OWN CUSTOM DESIGN!

SELF-LACING CHOCOLATE BREAD

Nothing is quite as cool as self-lacing sneakers, but this chocolate bread comes close. Plus it's kirgo delicious, which is something even the most bitchin' shoes can't claim to be.

YIELD: ONE 9-INCH BABKA LOAF

FOR THE DOUGH:

3 tablespoons butter, softened, plus 2 tablespoons, melted, and more for pan

2 cups all-purpose flour

2 cups bread flour

¼ cup unsweetened cocoa powder

1 tablespoon light brown sugar

1 tablespoon sugar

2 teaspoons baking powder

1½ teaspoons kosher salt

¾ cup milk

1 egg

FOR THE FILLING:

1 cup light brown sugar

1½ cups chocolate chips

1. Preheat the oven to 400°F. Grease and flour a 9-inch loaf pan, and set aside.

2. To make the dough: In a large bowl, combine the two flours, the cocoa powder, brown sugar, sugar, baking powder, and salt. Use a fork or your hands to cut 3 tablespoons of the butter into the flour mixture until it is the texture of wet sand. In a separate bowl, combine the milk and egg. Add to the flour mixture, and stir until a soft dough forms, then wrap in plastic and chill in the refrigerator for at least 30 minutes.

3. On a lightly floured surface, roll out the dough into an 18-inch rectangle about ¼-inch thickness, and brush with melted butter. Sprinkle dough with the brown sugar and chocolate chips, then roll up tightly like a jelly roll. Cut roll in half, then split each piece down the center, so you have 4 equal strips.

4. Line the strips up vertically, then pinch the tops together. Lift the rightmost strip over the two strips on its left, then take the leftmost strip and lift it over the two strips to the right. Continue braiding until you reach the end, then pinch the ends together, and use your hands to press the loaf together to tighten it up. Tuck the pinched edges underneath the babka, then place in the prepared loaf pan.

5. Bake 30 to 45 minutes, until golden. Let cool at least 15 minutes before serving.

BATTER UP BROWNIE SUNDAE

Take a swing at this futuristic dessert, where ice cream is replaced by gobs of brownie batter. The only thing you're getting clobbered by is tasty chocolate.

YIELD: 2 SUNDAES

2 cups flour

1 cup unsalted butter, softened

2 cups sugar

1⅓ cups Dutch-process cocoa powder

1 teaspoon kosher salt

6 tablespoons milk

2 teaspoons vanilla extract

1 cup semisweet chocolate chips

1 cup raspberry jam

½ cup heavy cream

1 cup white chocolate chips

Whipped cream, for garnish

1. Preheat the oven to 350°F. Pour the flour onto a baking sheet (shake it back and forth to make sure it's even). Bake 10 minutes, then let cool completely.

2. In the bowl of a stand mixer set to medium-high speed, cream the butter and sugar until light and fluffy. Slowly add the baked flour, cocoa powder, and salt, then add the milk and vanilla, and mix until everything is incorporated. Fold in chocolate chips with a spatula, and refrigerate 30 minutes.

3. In a small, microwave-safe bowl, combine raspberry jam and heavy cream, and heat in 30-second intervals, stirring in between, until smooth.

4. Scoop brownie batter into bowls and top each with raspberry sauce, white chocolate chips, and whipped cream. Enjoy this decadent treat!

GRIFF'S PITBULL COCKTAIL

Knock back a few of these fiery cocktails, and you'll be wired to chase a McFly around with a metal bat. Great-Great-Great-Great Grandpa Mad Dog would be proud.

YIELD: 1 COCKTAIL

1 ounce cinnamon whiskey

¾ ounce fresh lemon juice

1 ounce simple syrup

1 egg white

Bitters

1. Pour the whiskey, lemon juice, simple syrup, and egg white into a cocktail shaker (without ice). Shake vigorously for 1 minute, until foamy. Add ice and shake another 20 seconds to chill. Strain into a cocktail glass, top with a few drops of bitters, and serve.

CHICAGO CUBS WORLD SERIES—WINNING HOT DOG

It sure is tempting to want to think about placing a few bets on the Cubs when you have an almanac with all the stats and scores! What's even more tempting is a juicy, famous Chicago-style hot dog, especially when it's wrapped in bacon.

YIELD: 8 HOT DOGS

8 jumbo beef hot dogs

8 slices bacon

8 poppy seed hot dog buns or hoagie rolls

Ketchup, for buns

Spicy brown mustard, for buns

1 plum tomato, split, seeded, and cut into thin slices

Celery salt, for buns

8 dill pickle spears

½ cup sweet pickle relish

½ cup diced white onion

1. Preheat the oven to 400°F.

2. Wrap each hot dog with a strip of bacon, and secure the ends with toothpicks. Evenly space the hot dogs on a wire rack set over a baking sheet. Bake 10 to 15 minutes, depending on how crispy you like your bacon.

3. Split open the rolls, and warm them directly on the oven rack about 2 minutes. Spread ketchup and mustard inside the rolls, then line one side of each roll with tomato slices and sprinkle with celery salt. Add the pickles and bacon-wrapped hot dogs, dollop with relish, sprinkle with onion, and serve immediately.

RETRACTABLE FRUIT SALAD

For those of us who have yet to install a ceiling-mounted fruit robot in our kitchen, keeping a big bowl of fresh, sweet fruit salad in the fridge is the next best thing.

YIELD: ABOUT 10 CUPS

2 cups fresh pineapple, cubed

2 cups honeydew melon, cubed

2 cups red seedless grapes

2 medium mangos, peeled, pitted, and diced

¼ cup honey

¼ cup fresh orange juice

1 vanilla bean, split and scraped (optional)

1 cup fresh blueberries

1 cup fresh raspberries

1. Add the pineapple, honeydew, grapes, and mango to a large bowl. In a microwave-safe bowl, heat the honey in 10-second increments until runny, then stir in the orange juice and vanilla, if using. Pour over the fruit salad and toss well, then pour the blueberries and raspberries over the top. Serve immediately, or cover with plastic wrap and refrigerate if you prefer to serve your fruit salad cold.

SPICY REHYDRATED RAMEN

In the fast-paced future, we don't always have time for human servers or meals cooked from scratch. Food needs to be ready in an instant, but regular instant ramen is just *so* 20th century. Try this kirgo delicious noodle bowl when you want a taste of the future.

YIELD: 2 SERVINGS

¼ cup low-sodium powdered chicken bouillon

3 tablespoons hoisin sauce

2 cloves garlic, sliced thin

2 tablespoons Sriracha

1 to 2 teaspoons red pepper flakes (optional)

2 tablespoons dried chives

⅔ cup shredded carrots

½ cup kimchi

⅔ to 1 cup cooked shredded chicken

8 ounces dried rice vermicelli

1. Divide all ingredients between two 32-ounce mason jars, layering them on top of one another in the order listed. Fill the jar with boiling water until it comes ½ inch from the top, then let sit 5 minutes. Screw the lids onto the mason jars, flip them over, and let sit another 3 minutes. Shake well and serve.

MINI PIZZAS À LA 2015

The 21st-century working parent does not have the time to make an elaborate dinner for their family, but they can always depend on mini pizzas to be there in a pinch. These won't magically grow into family-size pies, but does it really matter when they're so much fun as mini pizzas? Plus, the classic combination of half pepperoni, half green peppers should satisfy both the meat lovers and the vegetarians at the table.

YIELD: 8 MINI PIZZAS

Eight 7-inch pita pockets

2 to 3 tablespoons olive oil

2 teaspoons garlic powder

1 jar tomato sauce of choice

3 cups shredded mozzarella

20 slices pepperoni, quartered

1 green bell pepper, sliced

1. Gently tug apart the two sides of the pita to loosen the pocket, making sure the bread isn't sticking to itself. Arrange pitas on a baking sheet or platter that can fit inside your freezer, and brush evenly with olive oil. Season each pita with garlic powder, then top with 2 to 3 tablespoons of tomato sauce. Spread sauce evenly across the pita, stopping at least 1 inch from the edge. Sprinkle an even layer of mozzarella over the sauce, then top half of each pizza with pepperoni and the other half with green peppers. Freeze 1 hour. (At this point, the mini pizzas can be wrapped in plastic and stored up to 2 months.)

2. Preheat the oven to 450°F. Put the desired number of frozen pizzas onto a foil-lined baking sheet, and bake 10 to 15 minutes, until the pita pocket has puffed up and the cheese is golden brown. Serve immediately.

BABY BACK ALMANAC RIBS

Going back in time might require a speed of 88 mph, but when it comes to ribs, low and *slow* is the way to go.

YIELD: TWO RACKS OF RIBS; 4 TO 8 SERVINGS

FOR THE DRY RUB:

1 cup light brown sugar

2 tablespoons kosher salt

2 tablespoons smoked paprika

1 tablespoon mustard powder

1 tablespoon garlic powder

1 tablespoon onion powder

2 teaspoons cayenne pepper

1 teaspoon black pepper

FOR THE RIBS:

2 slabs baby back ribs

1 cup yellow mustard

1½ teaspoons liquid smoke

TO MAKE THE RUB:

1. Put all ingredients for the rub into a small bowl; stir well to combine. Set aside 2 tablespoons to use later in the barbecue sauce.

TO MAKE THE RIBS:

2. Cut 2 long sheets of plastic wrap. Peel the membranes off the back of the ribs, place the ribs on the plastic wrap, and pat dry with paper towels. In a small bowl, combine the yellow mustard and liquid smoke. Use a spoon or pastry brush to smear the mustard mixture all over the ribs, then pack on the rub (remembering to reserve the 2 tablespoons you previously set aside), making sure every inch is coated. Wrap the ribs with 2 layers of plastic wrap, then refrigerate overnight.

3. Preheat the oven to 225°F. Line 2 baking sheets with foil, then place 1 rack of ribs on each. Remove and discard the plastic; cover each pan with foil, crimping well to seal, and bake 4 hours.

FOR THE BARBECUE SAUCE:

2 tablespoons reserved dry rub

½ cup light brown sugar

1 cup ketchup

½ cup apple cider vinegar

¼ cup yellow mustard

½ teaspoon liquid smoke

⅛ cup hot sauce

TO MAKE THE SAUCE:

4. While the ribs are baking, whisk together the ingredients in a small saucepan on medium-high heat. Bring the sauce to a boil, then reduce the heat to low, and simmer 10 minutes.

5. When 4 hours are up, remove the ribs from the oven; raise the heat to 425°F. Remove the foil, being careful not to burn yourself with any escaping steam, and brush the ribs with barbecue sauce. Put the ribs back in the oven, and bake another 30 minutes, brushing with more barbecue sauce every 10 minutes. Let the ribs rest 10 minutes, then serve.

TIP:
BE CAREFUL WHEN REMOVING THE FOIL FROM THE RIBS, AS THE ESCAPING STEAM CAN BURN.

If there's one cardinal rule of time travel, it's this: Do not mess with the timeline. Look where it got Marty: temporarily stuck in a terrifying alternate 1985 run by greedy, sleazy monster Biff Tannen. Everything the bully-cum–casino magnate touches becomes as rotten as he is, including Hill Valley. Here's a hot tip: If something catastrophic happens to our reality thanks to some immoral time-bending, head to the nearest casino, where you can eat your feelings at the buffet and everyone can feel like a winner.

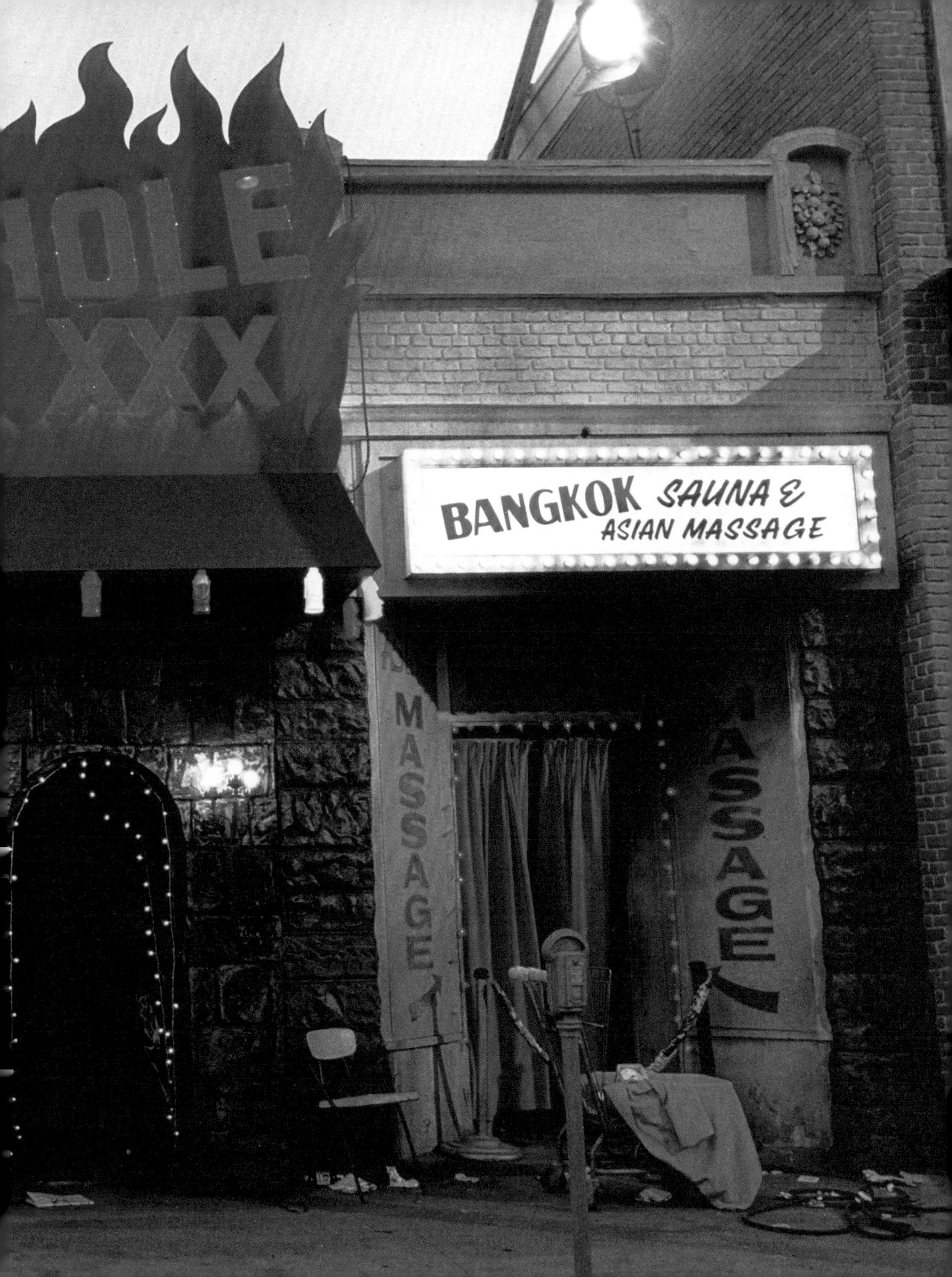
HOLE
XXX
BANGKOK SAUNA &
ASIAN MASSAGE
MASSAGE
MASSAGE

THE WORLD'S LUCKIEST SHRIMP COCKTAIL

What fun is being "the luckiest man on earth" if you can't show off like a big shot? Leave the tiny shrimp for the tourists at the casino buffet—when a real high roller orders shrimp cocktail, he wants the biggest, the best, the most beautiful shrimp anyone has ever seen.

YIELD: 4 SHRIMP COCKTAILS

2 large cloves garlic

¾ teaspoon kosher salt

3 tablespoons olive oil

2 pounds U-10 Extra Colossal shrimp, peeled, tails on, deveined

1¼ cups ketchup

⅓ cup horseradish

¾ teaspoon Worcestershire sauce

½ to 1 teaspoon Tabasco

2 large lemons, cut into wedges

1. Mince the garlic and salt together very well until they are almost a paste. Transfer garlic paste to a small bowl, and whisk in the olive oil. Toss the shrimp with the marinade, cover, and refrigerate 30 minutes.

2. Preheat a grill pan on medium-high. Grill the shrimp about 3 minutes a side, until the backs of the shrimp are opaquely white. Move to a plate to rest 5 minutes.

3. In a small bowl, whisk together the ketchup, horseradish, Worcestershire sauce, and Tabasco.

4. Divide the sauce among 4 cocktail glasses, then arrange shrimp and lemon wedges around the rims. Serve immediately or chilled.

QUICHE LORRAINE

Naturally Biff is a big fan of Quiche Lorraine, as it shares its name with the love of his life. This iconic, scrumptious dish is one of the most popular items at his breakfast buffet.

YIELD: 6 TO 8 SERVINGS

8 slices thick-cut bacon

6 eggs

1½ cups half-and-half

¾ teaspoon kosher salt

½ teaspoon black pepper

¼ teaspoon freshly grated nutmeg

6 ounces shredded cheddar

One 9-inch pre-baked pie crust

2 tablespoons finely minced fresh chives

1. Preheat the oven to 375°F. Lay out the bacon on a roasting rack set over a foil-lined baking sheet, and bake 20 minutes until crispy. Let drain on a paper-towel-lined plate.

2. In a medium bowl, whisk together the eggs and half-and-half until uniformly pale yellow and smooth—about 2 minutes. Whisk in the salt, pepper, and nutmeg.

3. Chop up the bacon, toss it with ⅔ of the cheddar, then spread out the mixture in the pie crust. Pour in the egg custard, then top with the remaining cheddar, and bake 35 to 40 minutes, until it barely jiggles in the center.

4. Let cool at least 30 minutes so the custard sets, then sprinkle with chives and serve warm or cold.

MAKE LIKE A TREE AND LEAF CHEF SALAD

You sound like a damn fool while saying it, but you don't feel like a damn fool for eating it.

YIELD: 4 SERVINGS

3 pieces deli-sliced roast beef

4 pieces deli-sliced cheddar

3 pieces deli-sliced Black Forest ham

4 pieces deli-sliced Swiss cheese

3 pieces deli-sliced turkey

4 ounces blue cheese

¼ cup mayonnaise

¼ cup sour cream

¼ to ½ cup buttermilk

½ teaspoon kosher salt

½ teaspoon black pepper

One 6-ounce package mixed salad greens

1 cup cherry tomatoes, halved

3 hard-boiled eggs, peeled and quartered

⅔ cup toasted pecans, chopped

1. Cut a 2-foot long sheet of plastic wrap, and lay it on the counter. Lay the roast beef slices end to end, overlapping by about 3 inches. Layer the cheddar on top, then add layers of ham, Swiss cheese, and turkey. Lift the bottom edge of the plastic, and use it to help you roll the cold cuts lengthwise like a jelly roll, then wrap tightly, and freeze 10 minutes to firm up.

2. In a medium bowl, whisk together the blue cheese, mayonnaise, sour cream, buttermilk, salt, and pepper. Pour half the dressing into a large bowl, then add the salad greens.

3. Remove the deli roll-up from the freezer, unwrap, then cut into ½-inch slices, and arrange on top of the salad greens with the cherry tomatoes and hard-boiled eggs.

4. Drizzle the remaining dressing over the top, and sprinkle with the toasted pecans.

HELL VALLEY CALAMARI FRIED DIABLO

Biff Tannen's Hill Valley might be a hellscape, but darned if that casino bar doesn't serve the crispiest, tangiest calamari around.

YIELD: 2 TO 4 SERVINGS

FOR THE CALAMARI:

1 pound calamari rings

1 cup milk

4 cups vegetable oil, for frying

FOR THE BREADING:

2 cups flour

2 teaspoons kosher salt

1 teaspoon black pepper

1 tablespoon Chesapeake Bay seasoning, plus more for seasoning

FOR THE DIPPING SAUCE:

2 tablespoons olive oil

2 cloves garlic, minced

1 teaspoon red pepper flakes

One 14-ounce can fire-roasted crushed tomatoes

1 teaspoon kosher salt

1. To prep the calamari: In a large bowl or resealable plastic bag, combine the calamari rings and milk. Refrigerate at least 2 hours or overnight.

2. When ready to fry, pour the vegetable oil into a large heavy-bottomed pot or Dutch oven on high heat. Clip on a deep-fry thermometer, and heat to 375°F.

3. Meanwhile, make the breading: Combine the breading ingredients in a large bowl.

4. Drain the calamari, then toss the rings in the mixture until well coated. Shake off excess, then spread out on a platter.

5. Working in batches, fry the calamari in oil about 3 to 5 minutes or until golden brown. Drain on a paper-towel-lined baking sheet. While hot, sprinkle with additional Chesapeake Bay seasoning.

6. To make the sauce: Heat the olive oil in a large skillet on high. Add the garlic and sauté until golden, about 1 minute. Add the red pepper flakes, and sauté another 30 seconds. Stir in the tomatoes, reduce the heat to medium, and simmer 10 minutes.

7. Serve the calamari hot with the sauce on the side.

THE NUMBER ONE CITIZEN

No self-respecting casino mogul would be seen drinking a typical martini. When you're Hill Valley's number-one citizen and America's greatest living folk legend, only gold-leaf cocktails will do.

YIELD: 1 COCKTAIL

1½ ounces good-quality vodka

½ ounce vermouth

Lemon twist, for garnish

Edible gold leaf, for garnish

1. Pour vodka into a cocktail shaker partially filled with ice. Set aside.

2. Pour a tiny bit of vermouth into a martini glass, and swirl around to coat the sides. Tear small pieces of gold leaf to decorate the sides of the glass, then pour in the remainder of the vermouth.

3. Stir the vodka 5 seconds, then immediately strain into the martini glass. Garnish with the twist of lemon.

CHICKEN CORDON BIFF

The ever elegant chicken cordon bleu was on almost every *très* gourmet hotel restaurant menu back in 1985. At the glamorous Pleasure Paradise Casino & Hotel, their version of this sophisticated dish, Chicken Cordon *Biff*, is accompanied by a very classy honey mustard dipping sauce.

YIELD: 4 SERVINGS

FOR THE CHICKEN:

4 slices Swiss cheese

Four ¼-inch-thick slices deli ham

4 boneless, skinless chicken breasts, trimmed

1 cup flour

1 teaspoon kosher salt

½ teaspoon black pepper

⅔ cup milk

2 eggs

4 cups plain panko bread crumbs

¼ cup grated Parmesan

1 teaspoon cayenne pepper (optional)

8 tablespoons butter (1 stick)

FOR THE SAUCE:

¼ cup mustard

3 tablespoons honey

½ cup mayonnaise

TO MAKE THE CHICKEN:

1. Lay out the slices of Swiss cheese on a clean surface, then layer ham slices on top. Roll each stack tightly to create 4 roll-ups.

2. Use a sharp paring knife to make a 1-inch slit in the side of a chicken breast at the thickest part. Insert the point of the knife nearly all the way through the chicken, then move around a bit to make a pocket. Stuff the ham and cheese roll-up into the pocket and seal with a wooden toothpick. Repeat with remaining chicken breasts.

3. Set up a breading station of shallow containers. In the first container, stir together the flour, salt, and pepper. In the second, whisk together the milk and eggs until smooth. In the third, combine the panko, Parmesan, and cayenne pepper, if using.

4. Dredge each chicken breast in the flour, eggs, and panko, and transfer to a plate lined with waxed paper. Refrigerate the chicken, uncovered, while you preheat the oven to 400°F.

5. Melt the butter in a large ovenproof skillet on medium-high heat, then add the chicken breasts and fry 5 minutes or until the undersides are golden. Flip the breasts, then slide the pan into the oven, and bake 20 to 25 minutes, until cooked through. Let rest in the pan 10 minutes before serving.

TO MAKE THE SAUCE:

6. Whisk together the mustard, honey, and mayonnaise. Serve on the side with the chicken.

BLACKENED FISH, THE EASY WAY

Cook this spicy blackened cod the easy way—on the stove—and we guarantee no major headaches. Fair warning: This flavorful dish is so tasty it just might knock you out.

YIELD: 4 TO 6 SERVINGS

1 tablespoon smoked paprika

1 teaspoon kosher salt

1 teaspoon fresh thyme leaves

1 teaspoon dry mustard

1 teaspoon cayenne pepper

¾ teaspoon crushed Szechuan peppercorns (optional)

1 teaspoon black pepper

Six 4-ounce Alaskan cod fillets

½ cup unsalted butter

2 tablespoons olive oil

1 lemon, cut into wedges

1. In a cake or pie pan, combine all the spices. Pat the cod fillets dry with paper towels, then dredge both sides in the spice mix.

2. Heat the butter and olive oil in a cast iron skillet on medium until the butter is completely melted. Cook the fish 3 minutes a side, until spices blacken and fish is cooked through.

3. Serve immediately with lemon wedges.

BIFF'S BANANAS FOSTER

If there's one thing a Tannen can't resist, it's playing with fire.

YIELD: 4 SERVINGS

¼ cup unsalted butter

¾ cup light brown sugar

¼ teaspoon kosher salt

1 teaspoon vanilla extract

¼ cup heavy cream

3 large bananas, cut into
1-inch pieces

½ gallon vanilla ice cream

2 ounces spiced rum

10 gingersnap cookies,
roughly crushed

1. Melt the butter in a large nonstick skillet on medium heat. Stir in brown sugar and salt; when the sugar melts and begins to bubble, stir in vanilla and heavy cream, and simmer 1 minute. Add the bananas to the skillet, and stir gently until they are completely coated in caramel, then turn off the heat.

2. Put a large scoop of vanilla ice cream into each of 4 serving bowls, and bring to the table.

3. Carry the skillet to the table, pour the rum over the bananas, and use a long-handled lighter to light it on fire in front of your guests.

4. When the fire goes out, pour the bananas foster over the ice cream, then sprinkle the crushed gingersnaps on top.

"THIRD TIME'S THE CHARM" CRÈME BRÛLÉE TRIO

For Biff, crème brûlée is a bit like ex-wives: Why have one when you can have three?

YIELD: 4 SETS OF THREE CRÈME BRÛLÉES (12 SMALL CRÈME BRÛLÉES)

12 egg yolks

¾ cup sugar, divided

5 cups heavy cream

1 teaspoon vanilla extract

2 ounces semisweet chocolate, melted

1 tablespoon instant espresso powder

⅓ cup raw sugar

1. Preheat the oven to 350°F.

2. In a large bowl, whisk together the egg yolks and half the sugar until completely smooth.

3. In a large heavy-bottomed saucepan on high heat, stir together the heavy cream and the remaining sugar. Bring the mixture to a simmer, then slowly pour in the egg yolks while whisking continuously. Remove the pan from the heat and strain into a bowl or measuring cup.

4. Divide the custard among 3 smaller bowls. Into the first bowl, whisk the vanilla; into the second, add the melted chocolate; into the third, add the espresso powder.

5. Bring a kettle of water to a boil. Place three 2-ounce ramekins into a baking dish, then fill each with one of the custards. Slide the dish into the oven, then carefully fill it with enough hot water to come halfway up the sides of the ramekins. Bake 25 to 30 minutes, until the custards barely jiggle in the center.

6. Remove the pan from the oven, and let the custards cool in the water 20 minutes before removing. Cover each ramekin with plastic wrap, and refrigerate at least 2 hours to set.

7. Just before serving, sprinkle the top of each custard with a thin layer of raw sugar. Caramelize with a kitchen torch, or slide under the broiler until the sugar is brown and bubbly.

TIRAMISU AL TANNEN

Serve these fancy tiramisus in long-stemmed wine goblets—it makes them easier to eat in a hot tub.

YIELD: 6 SERVINGS

8 egg yolks

1 cup sugar

1 cup milk

1 pound mascarpone

1½ cups heavy cream

1 teaspoon vanilla extract

3 packages ladyfingers, cut into 1-inch pieces

⅔ cup strongly brewed espresso

2 tablespoons coffee liqueur (optional)

¼ cup Dutch-process cocoa powder

1. In a medium saucepan on high heat, whisk together the egg yolks and sugar until well blended. Whisk in milk, and cook over high heat, stirring continuously, until mixture comes to a boil. Reduce the heat to medium, and boil gently 1 minute, then remove from heat, and pour through a wire strainer into a medium bowl. Whisk the mascarpone into the hot custard, then cover tightly with plastic wrap, and refrigerate 1 hour.

2. In a medium bowl, beat the heavy cream and vanilla to stiff peaks. Fold the cooled custard into the whipped cream in 3 additions.

3. Pour the espresso (and the coffee liqueur, if using) into a large, flat bowl. Working one at a time, dip the ladyfingers in the espresso for 1 to 2 seconds to soak and then layer them in the bottom of 6 wine goblets. You should use about half the ladyfingers, divided evenly among the goblets, for this first layer.

4. Top the ladyfingers with about half the mousse, dividing it evenly among the 6 goblets. Repeat this process a second time with the second half of the ladyfingers and mousse, then cover each goblet in plastic, and refrigerate 2 hours.

5. Before serving, dust with cocoa powder.

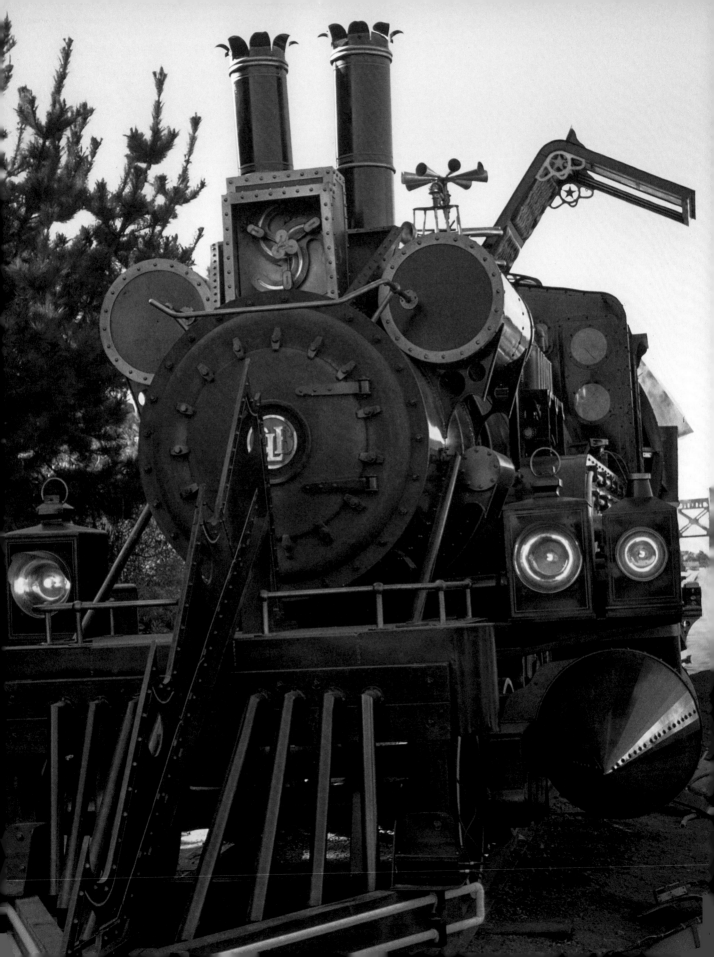

1885

Welcome to the Old West, when settlers came to California seeking gold in the hills of Hill Valley. Most homes don't have stoves, and no homes have refrigerators, but that doesn't mean there isn't good grub to be had. For the final stop on our era-hopping journey, here's a collection of recipes straight from the cookbooks of the day, slightly adapted for those of us who don't want to go hunting for rabbits for dinner.

DELOREAN WHITEWALL DOUGHNUTS

Fun fact: Ring-shaped doughnuts were actually invented in America in 1847, so it's fair to say Marty and Doc may have come across them during their Old West adventure. The whitewall tires on the DeLorean they find in the gold mine, on the other hand, could cause another time-splitting paradox if they rolled into the wrong hands.

 YIELD: ABOUT 24 DOUGHNUTS

FOR THE DOUGHNUTS:

6 tablespoons unsalted butter

4½ ounces semisweet chocolate

3 eggs

2¼ cups sugar

1½ cups buttermilk

1 teaspoon vanilla extract

1½ teaspoons kosher salt

4¾ cups all-purpose flour

½ cup unsweetened cocoa powder

4½ teaspoons baking powder

1½ teaspoons baking soda

4 cups vegetable oil

FOR THE ICING:

1½ cups powdered sugar

4 tablespoons milk

½ teaspoon vanilla extract

TO MAKE THE DOUGHNUTS:

1. Combine the butter and chocolate in a microwave-safe bowl. Heat in 20-second increments, stirring in between, until fully melted. Set aside.

2. In the bowl of a stand mixer set to high speed, whisk the eggs and sugar until pale and fluffy, about 4 minutes. With the mixer running, slowly stream in the melted chocolate mixture, then add the buttermilk, vanilla, and salt.

3. In a separate bowl, sift together the flour, cocoa powder, baking powder, and baking soda. Add the flour mixture to the stand mixer, and beat until just combined. Cover the bowl with plastic wrap, and refrigerate at least 45 minutes.

4. Roll out the dough on a lightly floured surface to ½-inch thickness. Use a doughnut cutter or cookie cutter to cut out doughnut shapes, and transfer to a baking sheet lined with parchment paper. Leave uncovered 20 minutes.

5. Add the oil to a large heavy-bottomed pot or Dutch oven fitted with a deep-fry thermometer, and heat on high to 375°F. Working in small batches, fry the doughnuts 60 to 90 seconds on each side until golden, then remove to a cooling rack set over paper towels to drain.

TO MAKE THE ICING:

6. Whisk together the powdered sugar, milk, and vanilla extract until smooth.

7. Dip the top of each doughnut into the glaze, let the excess drip off, then return to the cooling rack, and let sit until the glaze hardens, about 5 minutes.

HUNGRY BEAR CLAWS

These bear claws will look as delicious to you and your fellow diners as Marty does to a California black bear.

 YIELD: 8 PASTRIES

12 tablespoons butter, divided

2 sheets frozen puff pastry, thawed

¾ cup sugar

¾ cup light brown sugar

2 tablespoons cinnamon

½ cup honey

½ cup chopped walnuts

1. Melt half the butter by microwaving it in 20-second increments, stirring in between. Brush both sheets of puff pastry with butter.

2. In a medium bowl, combine the sugar, brown sugar, and cinnamon, and spread evenly across both sheets of dough.

3. Cut each sheet into quarters, then fold each quarter in half, pressing down firmly. Place the pastry on a cookie sheet, cover with plastic wrap, and refrigerate at least 15 minutes.

4. Preheat the oven to 400°F.

5. Use a sharp knife to cut four ½-inch slits into the unfolded side of each folded pastry square. Gently spread the "claws" of the pastry apart to make the signature bear claw shape.

6. In a small saucepan on medium heat, melt together the remaining butter with honey, stirring occasionally.

7. Brush the honey butter onto the bear claws and sprinkle with walnuts. Bake 20 minutes, then brush once again with any remaining honey butter. Return to the oven, and bake 5 more minutes or until golden brown.

SEAMUS'S ONE-SHOT POT RABBIT STEW

Life in the California frontier is tough, especially for hardworking immigrants like Seamus and Maggie McFly. But knowing your family's future is secure—and getting to put your feet up at the end of the day with a comforting bowl of rabbit stew—makes it all worthwhile.

 YIELD: 6 TO 8 SERVINGS

8 ounces thick-cut bacon, chopped

1 cup all-purpose flour

1½ teaspoons kosher salt

3 pounds rabbit meat, deboned and cut into large pieces

1 cup thickly sliced shallots

3 cloves garlic, minced

2 cups red wine

1 cup water

2 tablespoons blackberry preserves

2 tablespoons low-sodium chicken base

2 teaspoons herbes de Provence

2 tablespoons black pepper

2 tablespoons apple cider vinegar

3 tablespoons cornstarch

1. In a large Dutch oven on medium heat, brown the bacon until crispy, about 3 to 5 minutes. Remove bacon with a slotted spoon and drain on paper towels.

2. In a large bowl, combine the flour and salt. Dredge rabbit meat in flour, tossing well to coat, and shake to remove any excess.

3. Add the rabbit pieces to the Dutch oven one by one, being careful not to overcrowd the pan (work in batches, if necessary.) Sear the meat until dark brown on all sides—about 6 to 8 minutes—then remove to a plate.

4. Add shallots to the pan, and sauté until softened, about 2 minutes. Add garlic and cook 2 to 3 more minutes, until golden. Add red wine, using a wooden spoon to scrape the brown bits off the bottom of the pan. Stir in the water, blackberry preserves, chicken base, herbes de Provence, and black pepper, then return the rabbit and bacon to the Dutch oven. Reduce the heat to low, and simmer 1 to 2 hours, until rabbit is tender.

5. Whisk together the apple cider vinegar and cornstarch, then stir into the stew, and raise the heat to high. Cook until thickened, then remove from heat.

6. Let rest 10 minutes, then serve the stew over rice or mashed potatoes.

MAGGIE McFLY'S BISCUITS AND CIDER JELLY

TIP:
WANT TO STORE YOUR JELLY LONG-TERM? SEE THE INSTRUCTIONS FROM THE MANUFACTURER OF YOUR MASON JARS ON HOW TO HOT WATER PROCESS THE JARS. PROCESSED JARS CAN BE STORED IN THE PANTRY FOR UP TO TWO YEARS.

A recipe straight from the old country, these thick and hearty biscuits will keep your family happy and your stomach full whether you're city folk heading to the office or pioneers enduring a long day of grueling farmwork.

 YIELD: 4 PINTS OF CIDER JELLY; 10 TO 12 BISCUITS

FOR THE CIDER JELLY:

6 cups apple cider

1 cinnamon stick

½-inch slice fresh ginger

5 whole cloves

1 star anise

¼ teaspoon grated nutmeg

3 cups sugar

One 1.75-ounce package powdered pectin

FOR THE BISCUITS:

4 cups flour

1¾ tablespoons baking powder

2 tablespoons sugar

½ teaspoon kosher salt

1 cup unsalted butter (2 sticks), frozen

2½ cups buttermilk

TO MAKE THE CIDER JELLY:

1. In a large pot on medium-high heat, bring the apple cider, cinnamon stick, ginger, cloves, star anise, and nutmeg to a boil. Cover, turn off the heat, and let steep at least 15 minutes. Remove the spices and ginger with a slotted spoon; discard. Raise the heat back to high, and bring the cider to a boil.

2. Whisk together the sugar and pectin in a small bowl, then whisk rapidly into the boiling cider. Whisk continuously for 1 minute, then remove from heat and pour into sterilized mason jars.

3. Seal tightly, flip upside down, and let cool completely. Store open or unprocessed jars in the refrigerator.

TO MAKE THE BISCUITS:

4. In a large bowl, stir together the flour, baking powder, sugar, and salt. Grate the butter into the bowl using the large holes on a cheese grater; toss with your hands to make sure every piece of butter is coated in flour. Gently stir in the buttermilk until just combined (no dry spots visible). Cover in plastic wrap and refrigerate at least 15 minutes so the dough can hydrate.

5. Preheat the oven to 425°F. Line a baking sheet with parchment paper. Scoop tennis-ball-size biscuits onto the sheet, and bake 15 to 20 minutes until golden brown.

6. Let cool 5 minutes, then serve hot with cider jelly.

CLINT EASTWOOD'S COWBOY PUNCH

The classic cowboy punch recipe has about as much to do with the Old West as "Clint Eastwood's" cowboy shirt. It's a fine drink for junior cowboys and cowgirls, but if you're thinking of winning over some new friends at the local saloon, you may want to stir in a bottle of tequila.

 YIELD: 6 LITERS OF PUNCH

2 liters lemon-lime soda

1 liter club soda

2 liters white grape juice

One 750-ml bottle tequila (optional)

1 large orange, sliced

2 limes, sliced

1. Fill a large punch bowl with 3 cups of ice. Pour in the lemon-lime soda, club soda, grape juice, and tequila, if using. Stir to combine. Garnish with orange and lime slices, and serve.

MAD DOG'S CHICKEN AND DUMPLINGS

A true highwayman never robs a stagecoach on an empty stomach. A big pot of chicken and dumplings is just the thing to keep the entire gang fueled up and ready for the next hit on the Pine City Stage.

 YIELD: 4 TO 6 SERVINGS

FOR THE DUMPLINGS:

2 cups all-purpose flour

1½ tablespoons baking powder

1 teaspoon kosher salt

1 teaspoon black pepper

4 tablespoons unsalted butter (½ stick), melted

¾ cup buttermilk

FOR THE CHICKEN SOUP:

2 tablespoons olive oil

1 medium onion, diced

2 small carrots, diced

2 stalks celery, diced

8 ounces cremini mushrooms, sliced

6 cups chicken stock

One 10.5-ounce can cream of mushroom soup

Meat from 1 rotisserie chicken, roughly shredded

TO MAKE THE DUMPLINGS:

1. In a large bowl, combine the flour, baking powder, salt, and pepper. Add the butter and buttermilk, and stir until a soft dough forms. Cover with plastic wrap, and set aside.

TO MAKE THE CHICKEN SOUP:

2. Heat the olive oil in a large Dutch oven on high. Add the onion, carrots, and celery, and sauté until softened, about 3 to 5 minutes. Add the mushrooms, and continue to cook until everything begins to brown slightly, 5 more minutes. Stir in the chicken stock and soup. Bring to a boil, add the chicken, then reduce the heat to medium.

3. Use 2 tablespoons to scoop up golf-ball-sized dumplings from the dough; drop the dumplings into the broth. Partially cover the pot, and simmer 5 minutes. Check to make sure the dumplings are cooking evenly, flipping and moving them around as needed, then continue simmering until cooked through, about 5 more minutes.

4. Let sit 5 minutes off heat before serving hot.

EMMETT BROWN'S $80 BISCUITS AND RED-EYE GRAVY

If you have a highly active brain like Dr. Emmett Brown, it probably takes more than a cup of coffee to get you going. In addition to your morning joe, try smothering your biscuits in hot coffee-spiked gravy. If our calculations are correct, you'll be up and atom in no time.

 YIELD: 4 SERVINGS

FOR THE BISCUITS:

3 cups all-purpose flour, plus more for dusting

1½ tablespoons baking powder

1½ teaspoons kosher salt

¾ cup shortening

1⅓ cups buttermilk

FOR THE RED-EYE GRAVY:

¼ cup unsalted butter

⅓ cup all-purpose flour

¾ cup strong hot coffee

2 cups beef stock

2 tablespoons sugar

½ teaspoon kosher salt

1 small ham steak, diced

Chopped parsley, for garnish

1. Preheat the oven to 450°F.

TO MAKE THE BISCUITS:

2. In a large bowl, combine the flour, baking powder, and salt. Use the back of a fork to cut the shortening into the mixture until it achieves the texture of course sand. Stir in the buttermilk until a wet dough just comes together.

3. On a lightly floured surface, roll out the biscuit dough to ½-inch thickness. Using a biscuit cutter or large cookie cutter, cut biscuits out of dough and transfer to a baking sheet, placing them at least 2 inches apart. Gather the leftover dough, roll it out, and cut out more biscuits. Repeat this process until all the dough is used.

4. Bake biscuits 10 to 12 minutes or until golden brown. Remove to a wire rack to cool.

TO MAKE THE GRAVY:

5. Melt the butter in a large skillet on medium heat. Whisk in the flour, and cook until golden brown, about 5 minutes, stirring constantly. Whisk in the coffee, beef stock, sugar, and salt. Bring to a boil. Add the diced ham, then reduce the heat to low, and simmer until thickened, about 2 to 3 minutes.

6. Split the warm biscuits in half, then ladle the red-eye gravy over top. Garnish with chopped parsley and serve immediately.

THE PALACE SALOON BEEF JERKY STEW

Based on a real recipe from the Old West, this hearty dish uses fresh beef alongside traditional jerky. With twice the meat as your average beef stew, it makes a meal a cowboy would rides miles of dusty trails to enjoy.

 YIELD: 6 TO 8 SERVINGS

¼ cup vegetable oil

½ cup all-purpose flour

1 teaspoon kosher salt

½ teaspoon black pepper

½ teaspoon cayenne pepper

1½ pounds beef stew meat

1 large onion, chopped

3 carrots, chopped

4 ribs celery, chopped

2 cloves garlic, minced

2 tablespoons tomato paste

1 tablespoon chili powder

2 cups beef stock

8 ounces beef jerky

4 large russet potatoes, peeled and chopped

2 dried bay leaves

1 tablespoon balsamic vinegar

SPECIAL SUPPLIES:
Slow cooker

1. Heat the oil in a large skillet on high.

2. In a large bowl, combine the flour, salt, pepper, and cayenne pepper. Add the beef stew meat, and toss until well coated. Shake off excess flour, then add to the pot, and brown the meat well— about 4 minutes a side. Remove the beef to a slow cooker.

3. Add the onion, carrots, and celery to the skillet, and cook on high until brown, about 3 minutes. Add the garlic, tomato paste, and chili powder, and cook another 2 minutes, until fragrant. Transfer everything to the slow cooker.

4. Add the stock, stirring, then add the beef jerky, potatoes and bay leaves. Cook on low 8 hours, until the beef shreds easily with a fork. Stir in the balsamic vinegar, then taste the stew for seasoning, adjusting as desired.

5. Serve hot with crusty bread to sop up all the sauce.

FRISBEE APPLE PIE

Pies fly when you're having fun—or when you're trying to save your friend from a bully with a really tiny gun.

 YIELD: 6 TO 8 SERVINGS

6 Granny Smith apples, peeled, cored, and sliced thick

⅓ cup sugar

⅓ cup light brown sugar

1 teaspoon ground cinnamon

½ teaspoon ground cardamom

¼ cup all-purpose flour

1 teaspoon vanilla extract

1½ teaspoons kosher salt

1 package ready-to-use refrigerated pie dough (2 sheets)

1 egg

1 tablespoon water

1. Place the apples in a large microwave-safe bowl, and heat on high for 8 minutes. Let cool slightly, then strain out the excess juice. Return the partially cooked apples to the bowl, then toss with the sugar, brown sugar, cinnamon, cardamom, flour, vanilla, and salt.

2. Unroll the dough. Line a 9-inch pie pan with one sheet, then fill with the apples. Cover with the second dough sheet, crimp the edges, and cut small slits in the top to let steam escape. Freeze the pie 30 minutes.

3. Place a baking sheet on the center rack of the oven, then preheat to 425°F. When the oven is ready, place the pie on the hot baking sheet, and bake 15 minutes, then reduce the heat to 375°F, and bake another 30 minutes.

4. In a small bowl, beat together the egg and water to make an egg wash. Brush onto the pie, and bake another 5 minutes until set.

5. Cool at least 1 hour before serving.

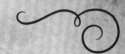

CLARA'S RED BEAN PIE

Though this pie might not be common today, it was one of the most popular desserts in the real Old West. Once you've tried it, you'll wonder why it ever went out of style. With pintos pureed into a custard with buttermilk, sugar, and spices, the unforgettable dessert makes as big an impression as Clara Clayton does on Doc Brown—minus the narrow escape from death.

 YIELD: 6 TO 8 SERVINGS

Two 15-ounce cans pinto beans, drained and rinsed

4 tablespoons (½ stick) unsalted butter, melted

¾ cup light brown sugar

1½ teaspoons kosher salt

3 eggs

1 cup buttermilk

½ cup quick-cooking oats

1 tablespoon vanilla extract

½ teaspoon ground cinnamon

½ teaspoon ground allspice

¼ teaspoon ground cloves

¼ teaspoon grated nutmeg

1½ tablespoons cornstarch

One frozen 9-inch pre-baked pie crust

1. Preheat the oven to 400°F.

2. In a food processor, pulse the beans, butter, brown sugar, and salt until broken down. Add the eggs, buttermilk, oats, vanilla, dried spices, and cornstarch, and puree until smooth.

3. Pour into the pie crust, and bake 15 minutes. Reduce the heat to 350°F, and continue baking until custard is mostly set, about 10 to 15 minutes.

4. Let rest at least 2 hours before serving, so the custard is fully set.

HILL VALLEY CLOCK TOWER INAUGURAL CHICKEN FRY

Celebrating a once-in-a-lifetime event like the raising of Hill Valley's famous Clock Tower requires a big ol' barn burner of a hootenanny. You're gonna need to scale this recipe up by about a thousand or so if you're planning to feed the whole town. As is, it's fun for a party of four.

 YIELD: 4 SERVINGS

FOR THE FRIED CHICKEN:

¼ cup plus 2 teaspoons kosher salt

½ gallon sweet tea

1 whole chicken, cut into 8 pieces (or 2 chicken breasts, 2 thighs, 2 legs, 2 wings, all bone-in)

2 quarts canola oil, for frying

3 cups all-purpose flour

1 teaspoon black pepper

1 teaspoon paprika

TO MAKE THE FRIED CHICKEN:

1. In a large container, stir ¼ cup of the salt into the sweet tea until it dissolves, then add the chicken to the brine. Seal and refrigerate overnight.

2. Clip a deep-fry thermometer to the side of a large heavy-bottomed pot, add the canola oil, and heat to 400°F. Preheat the oven to 375°F, then place a wire rack over an aluminum foil–lined baking sheet.

3. In a small bowl, combine the remaining salt, flour, pepper, and paprika.

4. Remove the chicken breasts from the brine, shaking off any excess, then dredge in flour until thickly coated and gently lower into the oil. Repeat with the chicken thighs. Fry the breasts and thighs until golden brown—about 10 minutes—then move to the rack and transfer to the oven.

5. Repeat with the wings and legs, adding them to the baking sheet in the oven after frying. Continue cooking until a thermometer inserted into each piece registers 165°F, 10 to 15 minutes.

CONTINUED ON PAGE 123 . . .

FOR THE COLESLAW:

½ cup mayonnaise

¼ cup buttermilk

2 tablespoons apple cider vinegar

Salt and black pepper

½ head green cabbage, shredded

¼ head red cabbage, shredded

2 medium carrots, grated

FOR THE LEMON HAYMAKER:

½ cup apple cider vinegar

¼ cup honey

⅛ cup molasses

1 teaspoon ground ginger

8 cups water

1 cup fresh lemon juice, from about 4 extra large lemons

TO MAKE THE COLESLAW:

6. In a large bowl, whisk together the mayonnaise, buttermilk, apple cider vinegar, salt, and pepper. Add the green cabbage, red cabbage, and carrots, and toss well.

TO MAKE THE LEMON HAYMAKER:

7. In a small saucepan on medium-high, heat the apple cider vinegar until just steaming. Stir in the honey, molasses, and ginger until dissolved.

8. Pour into a ½-gallon pitcher, and add the water and lemon juice. Fill with ice, stir, and serve.

STARGAZING STEW

There was no Town Theater for date nights back in 1885, but who needs movies when the cosmos puts on such a romantic show? Take some inspiration from Doc and Clara, and fall in love under the stars with a telescope, a cozy blanket, and a couple of thermoses full of this hearty mushroom stew to keep you warm.

 YIELD: 6 TO 10 SERVINGS

1 large yellow onion, diced

2 pounds cremini mushrooms, quartered

3 tablespoons olive oil

2 teaspoons kosher salt

3 cloves garlic, chopped

½ small fennel bulb, thinly sliced

4 carrots, chopped

2 large stalks celery, chopped

4 tablespoons tomato paste

1 teaspoon fresh thyme leaves

1 teaspoon black pepper

3 tablespoons instant flour

½ cup dry red wine

4 cups vegetable stock

2 teaspoons Worcestershire sauce

2 large dried bay leaves

4 cups Yukon Gold potatoes, diced

1. In a large Dutch oven on high heat, sauté the onion and mushrooms in olive oil with a pinch of salt until the onions are translucent and the mushrooms begin to turn deeply brown, 5 to 8 minutes.

2. Add the garlic, and continue cooking another minute or so until fragrant, then add the fennel, carrots, celery, tomato paste, thyme, the rest of the salt, and pepper, and cook, stirring occasionally, another 5 minutes.

3. Stir in the instant flour, then add the red wine, vegetable stock, Worcestershire sauce, and bay leaves. Add the potatoes, and bring the stew to a boil, then reduce the heat to low, and simmer 45 minutes. Serve hot.

EMMETT BROWN'S SARSAPARILLA AND PEAR MOCKTAIL

Looking for a delicious nonalcoholic drink to down in a fit of brokenhearted melancholy? Try mixing that newfangled health tonic "sarsaparilla" with a little pear and lemon. It may not cure all your blues, but at least you'll still be upright when it's gone.

 YIELD: 2 MOCKTAILS

⅓ cup chopped canned pears

½ ounce lemon juice

Dash grapefruit bitters

12 ounces sarsaparilla

Fresh pear slices, for garnish

1. In a cocktail shaker, muddle the canned pears, lemon juice, and grapefruit bitters. Slowly stir in the sarsaparilla, then strain between 2 cocktail glasses, and garnish with pear slices.

WAKE-UP JUICE

If you skipped the sarsaparilla mocktail last night and went straight for the whiskey, you might be in need of a glass of Wake-Up Juice—particularly if you need to be somewhere important in, say, 10 minutes. Fortunately, unlike the potent concoction that got Doc Brown back on his feet, this Wake-Up Juice—in which whiskey is encouraged but not required—is delicious. No clothespin necessary.

 YIELD: 4 TO 8 DRINKS

One 46-ounce can tomato juice

1 cup dill pickle juice

¼ cup horseradish

⅛ cup Worcestershire sauce

2 tablespoons fresh lemon juice, from about one large lemon

1 tablespoon celery salt

1 tablespoon cayenne pepper

2 tablespoons hot sauce

Big ol' glug strong whiskey (optional)

Celery, for garnish

1. In a pitcher, stir together the tomato juice, pickle juice, horseradish, Worcestershire sauce, lemon juice, celery salt, cayenne pepper, and hot sauce. Refrigerate at least 15 minutes—preferably at least an hour—for the flavors to meld.

2. Fill a pint glass halfway with ice. If desired, pour in a shot or two of whiskey. Fill the glass with the mix, and stir together with a celery stalk.

EIGHT O'CLOCK EGGS AND HASH

There are two things everybody knows about the Palace Saloon: It's the best place to catch an early morning gunfight, and they serve a mean plate of eggs and hash for folks to enjoy while they're watching the show. Make sure you get there early, though; word is, the action starts promptly at eight o'clock.

 YIELD: 4 TO 6 SERVINGS

Olive oil, for frying

1 pound ground pork sausage

1 white onion, sliced

2 green peppers, diced

2 jalapeños, minced

One 30-ounce package frozen diced potatoes, thawed

1 teaspoon kosher salt

1 teaspoon black pepper

6 eggs

¾ cup shredded cheddar

Salsa of choice, for serving

Hot sauce, for serving

1. Preheat the oven to 400°F.

2. Coat the bottom of an oven-safe skillet with a thin layer of olive oil, and heat until the oil begins to shimmer. Add the sausage, breaking into pieces with a wooden spoon, and cook until deeply brown, 5 to 7 minutes. Remove the sausage to a plate, then add the onion, peppers, jalapeños, and potatoes to the skillet. Cook, stirring occasionally, until the potatoes brown, about 5 minutes.

3. Add the sausage back into the skillet, season with the salt and pepper, then spread out so the bottom of the pan is completely covered. Crack the eggs on top of the hash, then transfer the entire skillet to the oven. Bake 5 to 15 minutes, depending on how well cooked you like your yolks.

4. When the eggs are about 2 minutes short of how you like them, sprinkle the hash with cheddar, then bake until it melts.

5. Serve immediately with salsa and hot sauce.

BULLETPROOF CAST IRON STRAWBERRY PANCAKE

Cast iron: great for stopping bullets, even better for making delicious oven-baked pancakes. Just remember to let your skillet cool completely before using it as armor. Cast iron *burns*.

 YIELD: 1 TO 2 SERVINGS

2 eggs

½ cup milk

½ teaspoon kosher salt

⅓ cup flour

¼ cup corn flour

3 tablespoons butter

1 pint strawberries, sliced

½ cup light brown sugar

1 teaspoon vanilla extract

Whipped cream (optional)

Powdered sugar (optional)

1. Place a 10-inch cast iron skillet in the oven and heat to 475°F.

2. While the pan is heating, beat the eggs in a medium bowl until pale yellow, then whisk in the milk, salt, flour, and corn flour. Carefully add the butter to the skillet in the oven, let it melt completely, then swirl around the pan so the bottom is completely coated.

3. Remove the hot pan from the oven, pour in the pancake batter, and bake 10 to 13 minutes, until puffed and light brown.

4. While the pancake is baking, combine the strawberries and brown sugar in a small saucepan on medium heat, and cook, stirring occasionally, until the sugar dissolves and the mixture begins bubbling. Remove from the heat, and stir in the vanilla.

5. Serve the pancake immediately with the strawberry sauce and, if desired, whipped cream and powdered sugar.

TIME TRAIN
TEA SERVICE

DeLoreans are pretty sweet, but oh, what it must be like to travel on a time train! Comfy beds to sleep in, giant picture windows to take in the scenery, long aisles for children to chase each other up and down, and an elegant dining car where you can enjoy a proper afternoon tea, no matter where (or when) you are.

 YIELD: 4 TO 6 SERVINGS

1985 COUNTRY CLUB TEA SANDWICH:

8 slices pumpernickel bread

4 ounces cream cheese, softened to room temperature

2 tablespoons minced fresh dill

1 small shallot, minced

8 ounces smoked salmon

1955 CANDIED PECANS:

2 tablespoons butter

1 pound pecan halves

1 teaspoon kosher salt

½ cup light brown sugar

3 tablespoons water

1985 COUNTRY CLUB TEA SANDWICH:

1. Cut the crusts off the pumpernickel slices so they form perfect rectangles, then toast.

2. In a small bowl, beat the cream cheese, dill, and shallot together with a fork until smooth.

3. Spread onto 4 slices of the toasted pumpernickel, add 1 or 2 slices of smoked salmon, and top with the remaining pieces of bread. Cut into rectangles and serve.

1955 CANDIED PECANS:

1. Melt the butter in a nonstick skillet on medium-high heat. Add the pecan halves and salt, and cook until aromatic, about 3 to 5 minutes. Add the brown sugar and water, and cook, stirring occasionally with a wooden spoon, until the liquid has mostly evaporated and the pecans are caramelized, about 5 minutes.

2. Pour the nuts onto a piece of parchment paper, and cool completely before serving.

CONTINUED ON PAGE 133 . . .

2015 FREEZE-DRIED-FRUIT SCONES:

3 cups all-purpose flour

⅔ cup light brown sugar

1½ tablespoons baking powder

1½ teaspoons kosher salt

⅔ cup unsalted butter, diced and chilled

2 ounces freeze-dried berries of choice

2 eggs

1 cup plus 2 tablespoons heavy cream

3 tablespoons raw turbinado sugar

1885 CALIFORNIA SUNSHINE TEA:

8 black tea bags

8 cups water

2 lemons, cut in half

⅓ cup or more of California honey

2015 FREEZE-DRIED-FRUIT SCONES:

1. In a large bowl, combine the flour, brown sugar, baking powder, and salt. Add the butter to the flour mixture, and use your hands to cut the butter into the flour until it is the texture of moist sand. Add the freeze-dried berries, and gently crush into bite-size pieces. Make a well in the center of the dry ingredients, then pour in the eggs and 1 cup of the heavy cream, and beat gently with a fork. Stir the wet and dry ingredients together to make a soft dough, then wrap in plastic and refrigerate at least 30 minutes.

2. Preheat the oven to 375°F. Line a baking sheet with parchment paper, and set aside.

3. On a lightly floured surface, roll out the dough out to ½-inch thickness. Use a biscuit cutter or paring knife to cut miniature scones in the shape of your choice. Gather remaining dough, reroll, and cut out more scones. Repeat until all the dough is gone.

4. Place the scones on the baking sheet, spaced at least 2 inches apart. Brush each scone with the remaining cream, then sprinkle with raw sugar, and bake 10 to 15 minutes, until golden brown. Remove to a wire rack to cool.

1885 CALIFORNIA SUNSHINE TEA:

1. Remove the strings and tags from the teabags, and put in a large glass jar with the water. Seal tightly, then put it outside in the sunshine to brew. Depending on how hot the day is and how strong you like your tea, this could take anywhere from 1 to 6 hours.

2. Once it's brewed to your liking, remove the teabags with tongs, squeeze in the juice from the lemons, and stir in as much honey as you'd like to sweeten.

HOSTING A
BACK TO THE FUTURE
MOVIE MARATHON

Back to back to back, *Back to the Future*, *Back to the Future Part II*, and *Back to the Future Part III* have a total run time of 5 hours and 42 minutes—the perfect length of time for a party! With a far-out menu and a little creativity, you can treat your friends to an all-day movie marathon that hops back and forth in time alongside Doc and Marty.

SETUP

Make sure you have plenty of room for your guests to relax around the television comfortably. Arrange couches and chairs to give everyone an unobstructed view, and create seating on the floor with pillows and blankets.

Serve your food and beverages buffet-style so your guests can graze throughout the party. Use sturdy disposable plates and bowls (perhaps in DeLorean silver?) so guests can eat from their seats during the movies. For a time-travel-themed tabletop, head to the local thrift store to find old serving dishes, tablecloths, and other retro decor.

Transport your guests to 1985 the moment they walk in the door! Play a mix of your favorite '80s tunes on the stereo, show some vintage MTV clips on TV, and pass out cans of ice-cold cola for everyone to enjoy while waiting for the show to start.

BACK TO THE FUTURE

Just before the movie starts, sneak out to the kitchen, and get ready to take the party back to 1955. Hide a Bluetooth speaker in the dining area, and play doo-wop hits at low volume.

Cover your buffet with a nice tablecloth (just like in the Baineses's house), decorate it with seashells, and place a big bowl of Enchantment Under the Sea Punch (page 55) in the center. Set out slider-size Pohatchee Drive-In Cheeseburgers (page 46) and Goldie Wilson Mayoral Tuna Melts (page 39). In the drinks area, put all the fixings for a DIY soda fountain, along with a bottle of spirits in case someone wants to add a little excitement to their egg cream.

BACK TO THE FUTURE PART II

You and your guests will need a break before starting the second movie, so why not take that break in the future? Put the "Scenery Channel" on TV, play some futuristic electronic music, and invite everyone into the kitchen to watch their Mini Pizzas à la 2015 (page 81) puff up in the oven.

While your guests enjoy the adventures of Marty Jr., get ready to swap out the wholesomeness of the 1950s for the sleaziness of Biff's 1985. Turn your table into a casino buffet with a platter of The World's Luckiest Shrimp Cocktail on ice (page 89) and tiny cups of Tiramisu al Tannen (page 101). When looking for decor, the tackier the better (think animal prints and gold lamé). Set out gold-lined martini glasses and a cocktail shaker so your guests can mix themselves a Number One Citizen (page 93).

138

BACK TO THE FUTURE PART III

There's one more time hop to go, all the way back to 1885! By now your guests will be in the mood for something hearty, like a bowl of Stargazing Stew (page 125) or Mad Dog's Chicken and Dumplings (page 113). Put a bottle of whiskey and shot glasses at the bar, as well as the accompaniments for Emmett Brown's Sarsaparilla and Pear Mocktail (page 126) for those who prefer something alcohol-free.

And, of course, it's not a party without dessert! End the triple feature with a sweet smorgasbord that spans 130 years of history, from the Frisbee Apple Pie of the Old West (page 117) to the Hoverboard Cookies of the future (page 71). The cookies also make a great take-home favor for when the movie's over and the bash's outtatime!

TITAN
BOOKS

144 Southwark Street
London SE1 0UP
www.titanbooks.com

Find us on Facebook: www.facebook.com/titanbooks
Follow us on Twitter: @TitanBooks

© 2020 Universal City Studios LLC and Amblin Entertainment, Inc. All Rights Reserved.

All rights reserved. Published by Titan Books, London, in 2020.

No part of this book may be reproduced, stored in a retrieval system, or transmitted, in any form or by any means without the prior written permission of the publisher, nor be otherwise circulated in any form of binding or cover other than that in which it is published and without a similar condition being imposed on the subsequent publisher.

Published by arrangement with Insight Editions, PO Box 3088, San Rafael, CA, 94912, USA.
www.insighteditions.com

A CIP Catalogue record for this title is available from the British Library.

ISBN: 978-1-78909-638-5

Publisher: Raoul Goff
Associate Publisher: Vanessa Lopez
Creative Director: Chrissy Kwasnik
VP of Manufacturing: Alix Nicholaeff
Designer: Lola Villanueva
Editor: Hilary VandenBroek
Editorial Assistant: Anna Wostenberg
Managing Editor: Lauren LePera
Production Editor: Jennifer Bentham
Production Director/Subsidiary Rights: Lina s Palma
Production Manager: Eden Orlesky

Food and Prop Styling by Elena P. Craig

Insight Editions, in association with Roots of Peace, will plant two trees for each tree used in the manufacturing of this book. Roots of Peace is an internationally renowned humanitarian organization dedicated to eradicating land mines worldwide and converting war-torn lands into productive farms and wildlife habitats. Roots of Peace will plant two million fruit and nut trees in Afghanistan and provide farmers there with the skills and support necessary for sustainable land use.

Manufactured in China by Insight Editions

10 9 8 7 6 5 4 3 2 1